An Introduction to Teaching in UK Higher Education

Covering everything you need to know about teaching within the UK higher education system, this book is the ideal introduction for anyone looking to start their teaching career.

A must-read guide for international staff new to teaching in UK higher education, this key text focuses on what is particular and often baffling to those who are new to higher education teaching in the UK. With practical tips and advice rooted in relevant theory, it is an invaluable resource to guide you through the initial teaching experience. Breaking down all of the aspects involved in teaching, learning and assessing in UK higher education, this book covers:

- The key features of UK higher education – particularly how it might differ from other systems
- How courses and the curriculum are designed
- How to support learning within your teaching practice
- Advice on marking and giving worthwhile feedback
- How to develop your own professional practice
- A full glossary of key terms

An Introduction to Teaching in UK Higher Education is a one-stop resource for those looking to begin a career in UK higher education. Particularly useful for new international staff, it will also be of interest to those looking to improve their teaching practice.

Nuala Byrne is an Associate Professor and PGCHE (Postgraduate Certificate in Higher Education) Director in the School of Education, University of Nottingham, and works across their UK, China and Malaysia campuses.

Christopher Butcher is a higher education consultant working with a number of institutions across the UK and Europe and is a former academic developer based in a Russell Group university.

Key Guides for Effective Teaching in Higher Education Series
Edited by Kate Exley

This indispensable series is aimed at new lecturers, postgraduate students who have teaching time, Graduate Teaching Assistants, part-time tutors and demonstrators, as well as experienced teaching staff who may feel it's time to review their skills in teaching and learning.

Titles in this series will provide the teacher in higher education with practical, realistic guidance on the various different aspects of their teaching role, which is underpinned not only by current research in the field, but also by the extensive experience of individual authors, and with a keen eye kept on the limitations and opportunities therein. By bridging a gap between academic theory and practice, all titles will provide generic guidance on the topics covered, which is then brought to life through the use of short, illustrative examples drawn from a range of disciplines. All titles in the series will:

- represent up-to-date thinking and incorporate the use of computing and appropriate learning technology
- consider methods and approaches for teaching and learning when there is an increasing diversity in learning and a growth in student numbers
- encourage readers to reflect, critique and apply learning in their practice and professional context
- provide links and references to other work on the topic and research evidence where appropriate.

Titles in the series will prove invaluable whether they are used for self-study, as reference material when seeking teaching recognition or as part of a formal taught programme on teaching and learning in higher education (HE), and will also be of relevance to teaching staff working in further education (FE) settings.

Other titles in this series:

Giving a Lecture
   From Presenting to Teaching, 2ed
   Kate Exley and Reg Dennick
Using Technology to Support Learning and Teaching
   Andy Fisher, Kate Exley, Dragos Ciobanu
Leading Learning and Teaching in Higher Education
   The Key Guide to Designing and Delivering Courses
   Doug Parkin
Small Group Teaching
   Seminars, Tutorials and Workshops, 2ed
   Kate Exley, Reg Dennick and Andrew Fisher
Developing Your Teaching
   Towards Excellence, 2ed
   Peter Kahn and Lorraine Anderson
Examining Doctoral Work
   Exploring Principles, Criteria and Processes
   Jerry Wellington

For more information about this series, please visit: https://www.routledge.com/Key-Guides-for-Effective-Teaching-in-Higher-Education/book-series/SE0746

An Introduction to Teaching in UK Higher Education

A Guide for International and Transnational Teachers

Nuala Byrne and Christopher Butcher with assistance from Heather Timm

LONDON AND NEW YORK

First published 2021
by Routledge
2 Park Square, Milton Park, Abingdon, Oxon OX14 4RN

and by Routledge
52 Vanderbilt Avenue, New York, NY 10017

Routledge is an imprint of the Taylor & Francis Group, an informa business

© 2021 Nuala Byrne and Christopher Butcher

The right of Nuala Byrne and Christopher Butcher to be identified as authors of this work has been asserted by them in accordance with sections 77 and 78 of the Copyright, Designs and Patents Act 1988.

All rights reserved. No part of this book may be reprinted or reproduced or utilised in any form or by any electronic, mechanical, or other means, now known or hereafter invented, including photocopying and recording, or in any information storage or retrieval system, without permission in writing from the publishers.

Trademark notice: Product or corporate names may be trademarks or registered trademarks, and are used only for identification and explanation without intent to infringe.

British Library Cataloguing-in-Publication Data
A catalogue record for this book is available from the British Library

Library of Congress Cataloging-in-Publication Data
Names: Byrne, Nuala, 1966- author. | Butcher, Christopher, 1951- author.
Title: An introduction to teaching in UK higher education : a guide for international and transnational teachers / Nuala Byrne and Christopher Butcher.
Identifiers: LCCN 2020030122 (print) | LCCN 2020030123 (ebook) | ISBN 9780367186067 (hardback) | ISBN 9780367186081 (paperback) | ISBN 9780429197161 (ebook)
Subjects: LCSH: College teachers, Foreign–Vocational guidance–Great Britain. | College teaching–Great Britain. | Education, Higher–Great Britain.
Classification: LCC LB1778.4.G7 B97 2021 (print) | LCC LB1778.4.G7 (ebook) | DDC 378.1/250941–dc23
LC record available at https://lccn.loc.gov/2020030122
LC ebook record available at https://lccn.loc.gov/2020030123

ISBN: 978-0-367-18606-7 (hbk)
ISBN: 978-0-367-18608-1 (pbk)
ISBN: 978-0-429-19716-1 (ebk)

Typeset in Perpetua
by River Editorial Ltd, Devon, UK

Contents

List of figures vi
List of tables vii
Series editor introduction viii
Preface xi
Acknowledgements xiv

1 Key features of UK higher education 1
2 Education in the UK 21
3 How students learn and what the implications are for teaching 43
4 Curriculum and course design 62
5 Teaching for supporting learning 82
6 Assessing and giving feedback 109
7 Supporting students 132
8 Ongoing development of your professional practice 153
9 Key terms, glossaries and abbreviations 179

References 198
Index 205

Figures

2.1	Term and semester dates example	38
3.1	Maslow's hierarchy of needs	49
3.2	Vygotsky's zone of proximal development	54
4.1	Dennis, course-design model	73
7.1	Blended model of student support	135
7.2	An example of a senior tutor network	144

Tables

1.1	Scale of UK higher education in 2018/19 (within the UK)	5
1.2	Frameworks for higher education qualifications	10
1.3	UKPSF dimensions	12
2.1	The National Curriculum in England	27
3.1	Defining features of deep and surface approaches to learning	46
4.1	Progression	65
5.1	Learning outcomes driving selection of teaching methods	84
6.1	Assessment terminology	112
6.2	Assessment methods – advantages and disadvantages	117
6.3	Typical marking scales	118
6.4	Example of grade descriptors	121
7.1	Support required through the student lifecycle, and implications for teachers	136

Series editor introduction

THE SERIES

The Key Guides for Effective Teaching in Higher Education were initially discussed as an idea in 2002, and the first group of four titles were published in 2004. New titles have continued to be added and the series now boasts 12 books (with new titles and further new editions of some of the older volumes in the pipeline).

It has always been intended that the books would be primarily of use to new teachers in universities and colleges. It has been exciting to see them being used to support postgraduate certificate programmes in teaching and learning for new academic staff and clinical teachers, and also the skills training programmes for postgraduate students who are beginning to teach. A less anticipated, but very valued, readership has been the experienced teachers who have dipped into the books when reviewing their teaching or referenced them when making claims for teaching recognition or promotion. Authors are very grateful to these colleagues who have given constructive feedback and made further suggestions on teaching approaches and shared examples of their practice, all of which has fed-forward into later editions of titles.

In the UK, the work of the Higher Education Academy (HEA), now part of Advance HE, in developing the Professional Standards Framework (UKPSF) on behalf of the sector, has also raised the importance of providing good-quality guidance and support for those beginning their teaching careers. It is therefore intended that the series will also provide a useful set of sources for those seeking to gain professional recognition for their practice against the UKPSF.

SERIES EDITOR INTRODUCTION

KEY THEMES OF THE SERIES

The books are all attempting to combine two things: to be very practical and provide lots of examples of methods and techniques, and also to link to educational theory and underpinning research. Articles are referenced, further readings are suggested and researchers in the field are quoted. There is also much enthusiasm here to link to the wide range of teaching-development activities thriving in the disciplines, supported by the small-grant schemes and conferences provided by Advance HE, the Society for Research in Higher Education, professional bodies, etc. The need to tailor teaching approaches to meet the demands of different subject areas and to provide new teachers with examples of practice that are easily recognisable in their fields of study is seen as being very important by all the series authors. To this end, the books include many examples drawn from a wide range of academic subjects and different kinds of higher education institutions. This theme of diversity is also embraced when considering the heterogeneous groups of students we now teach and the colleagues we work alongside. Students and teachers alike include people of different ages, experience, knowledge, skills, culture, language, etc., and all the books include discussion of the issues and demands this places on teachers and learners in today's universities.

In the series as a whole there is also more than half an eye trying to peer into the future — what will teaching and learning look like in 10 or 20 years' time? How will student expectations, government policy, funding streams and new technological advances and legislation affect what happens in our learning spaces of the future? What impact will this have on the way teaching is led and managed in institutions? You will see, therefore, that many of the books do include chapters that aim to look ahead and tap into the thinking of our most innovative and creative teachers and teaching leaders in an attempt to crystal-ball-gaze.

So these were the original ideas underpinning the series, and my co-authors and I have tried hard to keep them in mind as we researched our topics and typed away. We really hope that you find the books to be useful and interesting, whether you are a new teacher just starting out in your teaching career, or an experienced teacher reflecting on your practice and reviewing what you do.

AN INTRODUCTION TO TEACHING IN UK HIGHER EDUCATION: A GUIDE FOR INTERNATIONAL AND TRANSNATIONAL TEACHERS

I am so delighted to introduce the newest addition to the series, which aims to support colleagues who are new to teaching within the UK

SERIES EDITOR INTRODUCTION

higher education system, whether based within the UK or transnationally overseas. To craft this book, Nuala and Chris have used their combined experience of supporting new teachers in the UK, China, Malaysia and Singapore (to name but a few), leading projects to develop significant resources for international staff and conducting their own research into the issues these colleagues face. The resulting text is a treasure trove of everything you need to know to get started with a teaching career in the UK higher education system. The authors explain succinctly how universities work, how they are organised and how the teaching and assessment provision is designed, delivered and quality-assured. They provide useful guidance on all aspects of the UKPSF areas of activity in teaching and learning, and clarify expectations. At the start of each chapter, the authors identify which dimensions of the UKPSF are covered in that chapter.

As with other volumes in the series, the underpinning theory is made very evident, clear explanations are littered with examples and case studies, and each chapter includes a guide to follow-up resources for the interested reader. I am sure this text will become an important and valued support for many colleagues as they seek to understand and adapt to the new educational world in which they find themselves. I feel that we have recognised the need for this book for many years and its arrival is long overdue.

Kate Exley
Series Editor

Preface

The aim of this book is to support staff, postgraduate students, graduate teaching assistants and researchers who are new to teaching in a UK higher education (UK HE) setting either within the UK or in an international setting. Having both worked with new teachers in UK HE for many years, we are aware of how challenging this transition can be for all new teachers, but in particular for international teachers who are not familiar with the UK system. In contrast to other generic publications, this book explores in depth some of the key ways in which UK HE differs from other countries; i.e. support for students, assessment practices, teacher–student relationships, etc.

This book builds on the International Staff website, which became the one-stop shop for academic and personal support for international staff, offering support to assist staff and their families to settle into the UK and to gain an understanding of teaching and research in HE. At its peak 34 UK universities subscribed to the site, which sadly closed in 2013. Chris was awarded a National Teaching Fellowship (NTF) in 2005 and this was his NTF project; Heather Timm was the Project Officer from 2007–2013 and designed and developed the website.

The book is also informed by a survey of international teachers who were new to teaching in UK HE. The findings from our survey revealed that many new teachers felt they did not have the support they needed to teach in a UK HE setting and that assumptions were made about what they knew. Throughout this book, we have used the data and quotes from the survey to highlight the key issues identified.

Chapter 1, *Key features of UK higher education*, starts by clarifying terminology and looking at the scale of UK HE. We then identify and discuss the key features of UK HE, which we believe all teachers need to be aware of: regulation and funding; quality assurance; teaching qualifications and recognition; competition; equality, diversity and inclusion; and online and blended learning. So we think this is a must-read for everyone!

In Chapter 2, *Education in the UK*, we look at the UK education system. First, in terms of pre-university education and qualifications to help you understand the educational background of UK students and how the design of degrees builds on the earlier stages of education. Second, we build on Chapter 1 by providing further information about HE that we think you will find useful.

In Chapter 3, *How students learn and what the implications are for teaching*, we consider some of the main theories that are currently influencing teaching and learning in UK HE and what the implications of these are for teaching. We conclude the chapter with a list of the key things to consider when teaching.

In Chapter 4, *Curriculum and course design*, we ask you to think about the big picture of curriculum to set the context, and then focus down on how taught courses are designed, approved and, if needed, changed within the UK system. This draws on many of the key features of UK HE that were introduced in Chapter 1.

The title for Chapter 5, *Teaching for supporting learning*, emphasises our belief that it is the learning, enshrined in the intended learning outcomes, that should be guiding your selection of teaching methods. We ask you to think about: the teaching methods that you plan to use, why you would select them and what technology might be available to enhance what you do and so improve learning gain for students.

Chapter 6, *Assessing and giving feedback*, aims to provide you with a basic understanding of assessment and feedback in HE and then focuses in more detail on the aspects of assessment that new teachers are likely to be involved in; i.e. marking and feedback, etc.

In Chapter 7, *Supporting students*, we look at some models of student support and how these have developed. We then look at what support is offered at different stages of the student's journey, by whom and how you might be expected to be involved. We conclude the chapter by looking at how you might support specific groups of students.

Chapter 8, *Ongoing development of your professional practice*, is structured around three questions. First, how do you know that what you do is good enough? We look at the sources of evidence that you can draw on to reflect on your practice. Second, how can you get better? This includes a survey of the development opportunities that should be available to you to develop your practice. Finally, does quality get recognised? Here we consider the ways in which you can gain recognition for the high quality of your practice.

Our survey showed that many colleagues felt lost in a sea of unfamiliar terms and acronyms; Chapter 9, *Key terms, glossaries and abbreviations*, attempts to address this in three ways: (1) by defining the key terms that we use throughout the text, (2) by providing links to glossaries and resources that define all of the educational terms that you will encounter and (3) listing the most common abbreviations that are used.

Acknowledgements

We would like to thank our families and friends for their support and encouragement throughout the writing of this book. In particular Penny (Christopher) and John, Ciara and Ruairi (Nuala).

Special thanks go to:

> Heather Timm, in recognition for the tremendous job she did as Project Officer for the International Staff website from 2007–2013
> Prof Pamela Hagan, Senior Tutor at the University of Nottingham, for her comments and feedback on student support
> The PGCHE team at the University of Nottingham for acting as a sounding board for ideas, and in particular for Chapter 3
> Louis Harrison, Head of the Centre for English Language Education, University of Nottingham, for his comments on English language support
> Dr Kate Exley for her advice, feedback and support throughout the writing of this book and beyond.

A big thank you to all those who responded to our survey and provided us with such an interesting insight into their experiences of being new to teaching in UK HE. Your quotes have brought this book to life!

Chapter 1

Key features of UK higher education

[UKPSF: A4, K6, V1, V2 & V4]

INTRODUCTION TO THIS BOOK

The aim of this book is to support those new to teaching in a United Kingdom higher education (UK HE) setting either within the UK or overseas: international staff, early-career academics, postgraduate students, graduate teaching assistants and researchers. Having both worked with new international teachers for many years, we are aware that assumptions are often made about what new teachers know and understand about the context in which they are teaching. This can be challenging even for those who have been educated in the UK, and can be overwhelming for international teachers, especially when they are involved in teaching UK HE overseas.

To inform the writing of this book, we carried out a survey of international teachers who were new to teaching in UK HE. Responses from 89 new international teachers of 33 different nationalities were received. Of these, 59 were teaching in the UK, 28 in a UK HE setting outside the UK and 1 in both (1 did not state where they were). This included 56 lecturers, 17 PhD students who teach, 8 researchers who teach and 8 teachers in other roles. The main findings from the survey showed that many new teachers did not feel they had the support they needed to teach in a UK HE setting. In particular, they felt that assumptions were made about what they knew about UK HE, and the support they got was not tailored to international staff. We use the data and quotes from our survey to highlight key findings and issues throughout the book.

At the start of each chapter in this book, we have identified which aspects of the **UK Professional Standards Framework** (UKPSF) that chapter covers. The UKPSF (2011) is an internationally recognised framework for benchmarking success within teaching and learning support and is explained further in the *Teaching qualifications and recognition* section of this chapter and in Chapter 8.

In our opening line, we have listed the wide range of academics to whom this book is aimed, whose roles and responsibilities for teaching will vary considerably. Some of you may be lecturers with a full complement of teaching activities and duties (possibly including module leadership), others may have freedom to design classes but have the learning outcomes (see Chapter 4) and content prescribed, whilst others may be following fairly strict guidelines as what to do and how to do it but are interested in developing their role. We have tried to cover all contingencies, but this means that you may need to be selective about which chapters and sections you concentrate on. To help you, we have divided chapters into sections and clearly explained what we aim to cover at the outset of each chapter. In each one, we highlight key terms in bold and italics (like the UKPSF above) which we think are important and are defined in Chapter 9. At the end of each chapter, you will also find a list of further resources that we hope will be useful.

In addition, of course, you will have several other academic roles and activities to fulfil; be those research, administration, outreach, etc. We are only addressing the teaching role in this text and would suggest that if you need guidance/help with the other aspects, you talk to your head of school/department and find yourself a mentor (see Chapter 8 for more on mentors).

INTRODUCTION TO THIS CHAPTER

In this first chapter, we identify the key features of UK HE, which we believe all teachers need to be aware of. In the interest of clarity, we shall start by explaining what we mean by UK HE and **transnational education** (TNE). We shall then provide an insight into the scale of UK HE both within the UK and overseas (in TNE), and then look at the UK HE context and explore some of the key features, such as:

- Regulation and funding
- Quality assurance
- Teaching qualifications and recognition
- Competition
- Equality, diversity and inclusion
- Online and blended learning.

KEY FEATURES OF UK HIGHER EDUCATION

WHAT DO WE MEAN BY UK HIGHER EDUCATION?

The United Kingdom is short for the United Kingdom of Great Britain and Northern Ireland. The UK consists of four countries: England, Scotland, Wales and Northern Ireland, whose capital cities are London, Edinburgh, Cardiff and Belfast respectively. In terms of governance, overall responsibility rests with the UK Government (often, and confusingly, also described as the British government). However Scotland, Wales and Northern Ireland have their own devolved governments/parliaments (with homes in their capital cities) that are responsible for a range of issues including education. This is important, because you will find that the devolved powers impact considerably on educational provision in the four countries. Therefore, the policy and practices will vary depending on where your home institution is based.

In the UK, *higher education* refers to education that leads to the awarding of degrees. So when we talk about UK HE we are referring to HE provided by institutions based in England, Scotland, Wales and Northern Ireland. There are various bodies involved in delivering HE but the majority are universities, colleges or institutes of technology. These are collectively referred to as **higher education institutions** (HEIs) but often *universities* is used in a general sense, and we use these terms interchangeably in this book.

Global reputation of UK HE

UK HE has a reputation across the world for the quality of education it provides, and some universities rank among the best in the world (see *League tables* below for more details). According to the QS World University rankings (2020), three UK universities are in the top 10 universities and 12 in the top 100. The *Times* Higher Education (2020) World University rankings places four UK universities in the top 10 and 17 in the top 100, with the University of Oxford in first place and the University of Cambridge in third place. So there is no doubt that UK HE is held in high esteem and as a result attracts many international students to come to the UK to study for a degree. In 2019, the UK had the second highest number of international students behind the Unites States of America (Dept for Education and Dept for International Trade, 2019). It has also meant that UK HE is now offered in many countries around the world.

UK HE transnational education

HE transnational education (TNE) is defined as "the delivery of degrees in a country other than where the awarding provider is based" (Universities UK

International, 2019, p.5). Alongside the growth in international students coming to the UK to do a degree, there has been a significant expansion in UK HE delivered outside the UK over the past 30 years or so. According to Universities UK International (2019), this can take the form of undergraduate courses, postgraduate taught courses and postgraduate research, either part-time or full-time. UK HE is delivered in all except 15 countries, and the five countries with most UK HE TNE students are Malaysia, Singapore, Hong Kong, China and Oman (Universities UK International, 2019).

The manner in which the HE is delivered varies and can include an overseas campus (often called branch campuses), local delivery partnerships, distance/online learning or blended learning, which is a mixture of online learning and face-to-face teaching. The latter may be delivered by local staff at overseas locations or by staff flying out from the UK to deliver short, intense blocks of teaching, often called *flying faculty*. The first UK HE campus overseas was opened by the University of Nottingham in Malaysia in 2000. By 2017, over 40 UK HE branch campuses had been established across the world (Cross-Border Education Research Team, 2017). However, branch campus provision only represented 4.1% of UK HE TNE in 2017/18 with 56.5% being through students registered at overseas partner organisations, 21.4% studying through a collaborative (franchised) provision, 17% via distance/flexible learning and 1% via other arrangements (Universities UK International, 2019).

The advice and ideas in this book are aimed at supporting new international teachers who are either based at an HE institution in the UK or are involved in delivering UK HE in some form of TNE. We shall now look at what we know about the scale of UK HE and TNE.

SCALE OF UK HIGHER EDUCATION

The Higher Education Statistics Agency (HESA) collects and disseminates data about HE in the UK and is a valuable source of open data for all those involved in UK HE. According to HESA (2020), in 2018/19 there were 169 publicly funded universities and other HEIs in the UK; there were 2.38 million students studying at these institutions, an increase of 2% from 2017/18, and just over 217,000 academic staff. Table 1.1 shows the breakdown of numbers for England, Scotland, Wales and Northern Ireland.

KEY FEATURES OF UK HIGHER EDUCATION

TABLE 1.1 Scale of UK higher education in 2018/19 (within the UK)

	Publicly funded providers	Number of students	% of UK HE students	Number of academic staff
England	135	1,942,535	81.5%	179,895
Scotland	18	253,475	10.7%	23,580
Wales	12	132,205	5.5%	10,265
N. Ireland	4	55,755	2.3%	3,325
Total	169	2,383,970		217,065

(HESA, 2020)

Of the 2.38 million total students in 2018/19:

- 1.8 million (76%) were undergraduates and 0.58 million (24%) postgraduates
- 1.88 million (79%) were full-time students and 0.5 (21%) million part-time
- 1.9 million (80%) were UK students and 0.48 million (20%) were international students.

(HESA, 2020)

So the majority of students are full-time undergraduates and from the UK. There are, however, a significant proportion of international students, especially at postgraduate level. Of the 217,065 academic staff, 68% were from the UK and 31% from outside the UK with the nationality of the remaining 1% unknown. In addition to the publicly funded HEIs described above, there are also around 100 privately funded HEIs in the UK with just over 70,000 students in 2018/19. These are called **alternative providers** by HESA, and many are specialist colleges in dance, music, arts, theology and other subjects.

The current number of students in UK HE is a result of two major phases of expansion following government reviews in the 1960s and 1990s (see Chapter 2 for further information). The 2.38 million students in 2018/19 equates to an approximate eleven-fold increase from 216,000 in 1962/63 (Robbins, 1963). Following the initial rapid increase in the 1960s, there was another rapid increase in the 1990s, which is often described as the shift from elite to mass HE. In 1963 about 7% of 18-year-olds entered HE; this rose to about 19% in 1990 and then jumped to 32% by 1995, when institutions called **polytechnics** (see Chapter 2) became universities (Dearing, 1997). In 2017/18 just over 50% of 18- to 30-year-olds in the UK participated in HE, reaching the target set by the Labour government in the late 1990s (see Chapter 2 for a brief history). So, it is not just the current scale that is important but also the extent that HE has expanded over the last 50–60 years.

In terms of UK HE TNE, in 2018/19 there were 142 providers with almost 667,000 students, 13% of whom were studying within the European Union and 87% outside (HESA, 2020). This means that over 85% of UK HE providers have some form of TNE. It is important to note that almost 39% of the total students were registered at one university, Oxford Brookes, on chartered accountancy programmes. There does not seem to be any data on how many teaching staff are involved in TNE, which is not surprising given the range of countries and diversity of provision.

REGULATION AND FUNDING OF UK HE

There are three main elements to HE in the UK: teaching and learning; research; and **knowledge exchange**, which refers to the exchange of knowledge and expertise between researchers and users of that research in society. The relative emphasis on these aspects varies depending on the nature of the institution, with some focusing predominantly on teaching and others placing a greater emphasis on research.

Regulation

As explained above, HE is one policy area where responsibility is devolved from the UK government to the governments in Scotland, Wales and Northern Ireland. As a result, the manner in which each country manages their HE varies, and hence there are four different HE funding and regulatory bodies:

- The Office for Students (OfS) is the independent regulator of, and allocates funding to, HE institutions in England.
- The Scottish Funding Council is responsible for HE in Scotland.
- The Higher Education Funding Council for Wales (HEFCW) is the regulator for funding and quality of HE in Wales.
- The Department of the Economy (NI) is responsible for all aspects of HE, including funding, in Northern Ireland.

This means that for some aspects of HE, such as tuition fees, there are different policies and approaches in the four countries, whereas for other aspects, such as quality assurance, there is a more coherent approach across the UK.

Although not a regulation or funding body, **Advance HE** is an important organisation to be aware of. Advance HE aims to enhance the professional practice of HE and improve outcomes for students, staff and society. Advance HE provides advice, support and accreditation related to teaching and learning, leadership and management, and equality, diversity and inclusion (see later section).

Institutional-level funding

UK HEIs receive income from a variety of sources, including students, government, charities and businesses, and many are themselves charities often receiving substantial philanthropic donations. The total income of UK HEIs in 2017/18 was £38.2 billion, £21.1 billion of which related to teaching activities, 8.2 billion to research, £4.5 billion to knowledge-exchange activities and the remaining £4.4 billion from other sources (Universities UK, 2019). The relative income from the three strands of activity will vary depending on the type of institution you work for, but it is clear that teaching and learning activities are the main source of income for UK HEIs.

The massive expansion of HE has led to significant changes to both the physical infrastructure of institutions and the ways in which they work. There has been investment in buildings such as accommodation, teaching facilities, libraries, health centres and sports facilities. There have also been considerable changes to how student support is managed at many institutions. In terms of teaching, class sizes have increased, with lectures often taking place in huge lecture theatres (in some cases for up to 500 students) and multiple runs of small group teaching sessions such as seminars, tutorials and laboratory classes. Changes to the curriculum, and assessment in particular, have been made to accommodate the larger student numbers. There is increased use of technology and **virtual learning environments** (VLEs) to enable more online or blended learning to take place. Many of these issues will be referred to in later chapters of this book.

Student tuition fees

From the early 1960s until the late 1990s HE was free for UK students studying in the UK. Tuition fees were paid by the state, and students were offered maintenance grants for living expenses. Following the Dearing review of HE in 1997, student tuition fees were first introduced in the UK in September 1998 and originally set at £1,000 per year. These have gradually increased but the approach and level of fees varies in the four countries of the UK. As of 2019/20, the tuition fees were £9,250 per year for home students in England, £9,000 in Wales and £4,275 in Northern Ireland, but tuition fees were abolished in Scotland in 2008 and hence there are no fees for home students in Scotland. The different approaches to funding are likely to influence students' choice of universities. Scottish students are more likely to stay in Scotland to do a degree with no tuition fees than to study in England, where they will have to pay £9,250 per year.

The tuition fees for international students tend to be a lot higher than for home students and vary considerably depending on the institution and the subject being studied. So, for example, laboratory-based or clinical course fees tend to be much higher than classroom-based courses. For UK HE TNE, fees will depend on the local country regulations, provider and type of course, so will vary considerably from one country to another.

QUALITY ASSURANCE

Quality Assurance Agency (QAA)

Quality assurance (approving to a minimum standard) and *quality enhancement* (making courses better) has been high on the agenda of UK HE. Currently the QAA (www.qaa.ac.uk) is the national driving force and its guidance, the **Quality Code**, comprises four major sections:

1. **Subject Benchmark Statements**: we discuss those briefly below
2. Qualifications and Credit Frameworks: we discuss the qualifications frameworks below and return to in Chapter 4, and credits are an important part of Chapter 4
3. Advice and Guidance: this is divided into 12 themes and includes guiding principles, practical advice and further resources; check them out
4. Supporting Resources: more really useful materials; check them out.

We will outline the important sections of the Quality Code in this chapter, and this information will provide context and background to other chapters in this book. As well as providing the national framework for quality assurance and enhancement, the QAA also inspects the quality of HE in England, Scotland and Wales (Northern Ireland has its own approach) and carries out TNE reviews. This means that every provider of HE will be measured against quality-assurance measures on a regular basis and given a grade. The result of this is that every HEI will have a quality unit of some sort; find yours and see what it does and expects. This means that there is a local interpretation of the national guidance, so you do not need to read all of the QAA information and guidance; you just need to know and follow your institutional processes.

Frameworks for higher education qualifications of UK degree-awarding bodies

There are two frameworks that apply in the UK (QAA, 2014) and they come under the auspices of the QAA: (1) the FHEQ – Framework for Higher Education Qualifications in England, Wales and Northern Ireland; and (2) the FQHEIS – Framework for Qualifications of Higher Education Institutions in Scotland.

The frameworks, and how they relate to each other, are shown in Table 1.2. The numbers in the table are referred to as *levels*, and *level* is important. We talk about a *Level 4* course and a *first-year* student; the distinction is that *level* describes the intellectual demand of the course whilst *year* refers to the chronological order that students attend the course. We mention this as you might find, particularly for resources and/or staff issues, that second- and third-year undergraduates attend the same Level 6 course as it is only offered every two years, or final/third-year undergraduates attend a Level 7 course with master's students. *Level* and *year* are different when thinking about UK HE.

You will notice that neither framework starts at 1, as they build on the qualifications and education stages that pupils in the UK attend prior to attending HE (see Chapter 2).

Thinking about qualifications, each one in the frameworks must have a clear statement about what is needed in order for a student to gain the award, and these are called ***programme (of study) specifications***. These are definitive records of each approved programme or qualification and their intended learning outcomes. This definition introduces another term – ***learning outcome*** – and we will return to that in chapters 3 and 4. The important point at this stage is that for any course that leads to a qualification that you are teaching on, there should be a programme specification and you should be familiar with that document as it will give you an overview of what is expected of your students in order to succeed and graduate with the award/qualification.

KEY FEATURES OF UK HIGHER EDUCATION

TABLE 1.2 Frameworks for higher education qualifications

Typical qualification awarded	FHEQ	FQHEIS
Doctoral degrees	8	12
Master's degrees	7	11
Primary qualifications in medicine, dentistry and veterinary science		
Postgraduate diplomas		
Postgraduate certificates		
Bachelor degrees with honours	6	10
Bachelor degrees		9
Graduate diplomas		
Graduate certificates		
Foundation degrees	5	NA
Diplomas of higher education		8
Higher national diplomas		NA
Higher national certificates	4	NA
Certificates of higher education		7

(Adapted from QAA, 2014)

Subject benchmark statements

The QAA states that subject benchmark statements

> describe the nature of study and the academic standards expected of graduates in specific subject areas. They show what graduates might reasonably be expected to know, do and understand at the end of their studies.
>
> (QAA, 2020)

They are written by subject specialists, updated periodically and cover both undergraduate (bachelor degrees with honours) and postgraduate (master's degrees) qualifications. They must be used as reference points when designing programmes of study but they are not intended to be limiting or seen as a national curriculum for the subject. Typically, a benchmark statement will include:

- General aims of the degree subject
- Baseline subject knowledge and understanding
- Expected attributes and skills, including professional skills
- Advice on teaching, learning and assessment in the discipline.

They may also include ideas of expected standards at different grades (e.g. pass level and upper second – see Chapter 6) which helps us set comparative standards across similar qualifications in different institutions. Read the statement that applies to your subject at www.qaa.ac.uk/quality-code/subject-benchmark-statements.

Teaching Excellence and Student Outcomes Framework

The *Teaching Excellence and Student Outcomes Framework* (TEF) was introduced as a pilot scheme in 2016 by the government in England and has continued ever since. It covers undergraduate teaching and aims to assess excellence in teaching and the quality of outcomes for students in terms of employment or further study. Participating institutions receive a gold, silver or bronze award which is valid for three years and reflects the excellence of their teaching, learning environment and student outcomes. The process is managed by the OfS in England, and participation was voluntary up until 2020. A subject-level TEF has also been trialled and a review of the TEF is currently being carried out. It is envisaged that the future TEF will be compulsory for all HEIs in England and optional for HEIs in Scotland, Wales and Northern Ireland. It is important to note that it is the QAA and relevant bodies within the four countries of the UK that are responsible for ensuring national standards for HE are met. The TEF looks at what institutions are doing in addition to those standards. TEF results are published on various websites and are likely to influence students' choices about where they study.

TEACHING QUALIFICATIONS AND RECOGNITION

A government review of HE in the late 1990s (Dearing, 1997) recommended the introduction of training for teaching staff on how to teach. As a result, most institutions run a variety of teaching and learning courses and workshops to support all those involved in teaching. Many run a postgraduate certificate-type course in teaching and learning, HE, academic practice (or similarly named courses) which are often compulsory for new academics (see Chapter 8 for further details). Alongside this, there is often optional or compulsory training for researchers and PhD students who teach. Most of these courses will have been guided by the UKPSF mentioned at the start of this chapter. The UKPSF is managed and led by Advance HE and is divided into three sets of dimensions, as shown in Table 1.3. At the start of each chapter in this book, we have identified which areas of activity, core knowledge and professional values are covered in that chapter.

The framework also enables individuals to gain formal recognition for their approach to teaching and learning against four different descriptors.

TABLE 1.3 UKPSF dimensions

Areas of activity	Core knowledge	Professional values
A1 Design and plan learning activities and/or programmes of study	K1 The subject material	V1 Respect individual learners and diverse learning communities
A2 Teach and/or support learning	K2 Appropriate methods for teaching, learning and assessing in the subject area and at the level of the academic programme	V2 Promote participation in higher education and equality of opportunity for learners
A3 Assess and give feedback to learners		
A4 Develop effective learning environments and approaches to student support and guidance	K3 How students learn, both generally and within their subject/disciplinary area(s)	V3 Use evidence-informed approaches and the outcomes from research, scholarship and continuing professional development
	K4 The use and value of appropriate learning technologies	
A5 Engage in continuing professional development in subjects/disciplines and their pedagogy, incorporating research, scholarship and the evaluation of professional practices	K5 Methods for evaluating the effectiveness of teaching	V4 Acknowledge the wider context in which higher education operates, recognising the implications for professional practice
	K6 The implications of quality assurance and quality enhancement for academic and professional practice with a particular focus on teaching	

(UKPSF, 2011)

This can be done either by completing an accredited course or, for experienced teachers, by submitting an application. There is further information about how this works in Chapter 8.

In 2014, HESA started collecting and publishing data on the number of teaching staff at each HEI who are *qualified* to teach. In its definition, HESA includes both teaching qualifications (postgraduate certificate-type qualifications) and teaching recognition (against the UKPSF) as teaching qualifications, although it does distinguish between the different ways in which this can be achieved. These numbers are often translated into percentages and used in league tables and websites (see next section) to help students decide which institutions to apply for. They have also been used by institutions to set targets for teaching staff to gain qualifications or recognition to enhance the institutions' teaching-qualification data.

Although HESA has no jurisdiction over UK TNE, many institutions that operate overseas have the same expectations of their staff there in terms of training and qualifications for teaching. So depending on your teaching role you may be required or encouraged to complete a course or gain teaching recognition. Even if not required, it is worth finding out what is available to support you in your teaching role (see Chapter 8 for more advice).

COMPETITION

Alongside the expansion in student numbers, the number of HEIs has expanded and the competition for students has really intensified over the last 10–20 years. This has led to an increase in the marketisation of HE. According to the *Guardian* newspaper (Hall and Weale, 2019), universities are spending hundreds of thousands of pounds on marketing as the competition for students increases. This includes digital advertising, social media and adverts on billboards and buses, and in some cases amounts to over £3 million per year. Institutions have become much more business-like and try to ensure that they have something distinctive to offer, such as degrees relating to research areas, links to industry, work placements for all students and flexible degree courses. The competition for students has also resulted in the greater prevalence of student surveys, league tables and university comparison websites.

Student surveys

The **National Student Survey** (NSS) was introduced in 2005 and is an annual census of final-year undergraduate students (around half a million students) at all publicly funded HEIs in the UK (www.thestudentsurvey.com). Its purpose is to gather student feedback to inform applicant choice, provide information about the student learning experience and provide public assurance. The survey contains 27 questions in the following categories, with the final one being an overall satisfaction score:

- The teaching on my course
- Learning opportunities
- Assessment and feedback
- Academic support
- Organisation and management
- Learning resources
- Learning community
- Overall satisfaction.

Data from the NSS is published in league tables and used in other evaluations, such as the TEF discussed earlier in this chapter. Similar surveys have been developed and are administered by Advance HE for postgraduate students on taught courses and postgraduate research students (see Chapter 8 for further information). These latter surveys are available for use in international settings, which is not the case for the NSS. There are, however, various other surveys that can be used in an international setting, such as the Student Barometer (see Chapter 8). Irrespective of the survey tool being used, it is clear that the results of these surveys are critical in terms of institutional marketing and enhancement of the student learning experience and are used by prospective students to inform their choice of where to study.

League tables

Another way in which HEIs are judged, and therefore a source of comparison data for prospective students and their parents, is league tables. There are three main UK HE league tables:

- The *Times* and *Sunday Times* Good University Guide
- The *Guardian* University Guide
- The Complete University Guide.

The criteria that each of these use to rank HEIs vary as the emphasis they place on different aspects varies. Most HEIs will be concerned about their absolute ranking but also their relative ranking compared to their local (geographical) competitors and to those of a similar type of institution. Like the student surveys, these rankings can drive teaching and learning-enhancement agendas within universities and colleges as well as informing student choice.

EQUALITY, DIVERSITY AND INCLUSION

A major focus of UK HE is currently on the issue of **equality, diversity and inclusion**. Equality or equity is about *treating everyone fairly*, diversity about *recognising that difference is positive* and inclusivity about *including people who might otherwise be excluded*.

Equality Act 2010

The Equality Act came into effect in Great Britain (not Northern Ireland) in 2010 and made it illegal to discriminate against someone on the basis of the following protected characteristics:

- Age
- Disability
- Gender reassignment
- Marriage and civil partnership
- Pregnancy and maternity
- Race
- Religion or belief
- Sex
- Sexual orientation.

(Equality Act, 2010)

As part of the Act, the Public Sector Equality Duty places a duty on all public sector bodies (including HEIs) to:

- Eliminate discrimination, harassment, victimisation
- Advance equality of opportunity
- Foster good relations.

(Advance HE, 2020)

Institutions are expected to make reasonable adjustments for staff and students with a disability. So for students this might mean having a note-taker in

KEY FEATURES OF UK HIGHER EDUCATION

lessons or extra time for exams or alternative assessments. However, there is a move towards designing inclusive assessments which would remove any need for adjustments. The term *inclusive teaching* is used to describe teaching in a way that enables all students to participate and fulfil their potential by removing any barriers that prevent students from learning. Another book in this series (Butcher et al., 2020) has a whole chapter on learning materials and resources for diverse learners that is worth reading.

Northern Ireland has its own Equality Commission, which is a non-departmental public body responsible for equality issues and provides protection against discrimination on the grounds of similar characteristics as outlined above. A link to its website is provided in *Further resources*.

Student diversity

Given the massive expansion in HE over the last few decades, it is unsurprising that the diversity of students studying for degrees in the UK has increased. In the early years, UK HE was the privilege of wealthy males who could afford a private education, but this has changed gradually and the percentage of female students is now greater than males, with 57% of students in 2018/19 being female (HESA, 2020). International students now make up around 20% of the student population. However, concerns regarding the under-representation of particular UK groups, such as those from low-income households, disadvantaged backgrounds and certain ethnic groups, as well as students with a disability, has led to *widening participation* efforts being high on the agenda of HE regulators and funding bodies. Various targets have been set and widening-participation data is collected and reported by a range of bodies and institutions. Most HE institutions have widening-participation units who tend to run outreach activities with local schools to raise aspirations and support progression to HE, as well as targeted widening-participation activities for under-represented groups. Whilst progress has been made on some fronts with more disabled students and certain ethnic groups, particularly black people, entering HE, a government report on HE student numbers (Bolton, 2020) has highlighted a number of issues:

- The number of part-time students almost halved between 2009/10 and 2018/19 compared to a 12% increase in full-time students.
- Only 13% of white male 18-year-olds from "low participation households" enter HE.
- Only 3.1% of 18-year-olds from low-income families got into a "prestigious" university in 2019 compared to 10.4% of

16

higher-income families (see Chapter 2 for more information about different types of universities).

The widening-participation issues and approaches vary across the four UK countries. As an example, in England, the OfS requires each HEI to produce an ***access and participation plan***, which outlines how they will improve equality of opportunity. Progress against this plan is monitored by the OfS and there are sanctions for any breaches. Although the approach taken varies across the four countries, they all involve data collection and analysis, target-setting and monitoring of achievement of those targets. One of the OfS objectives sums up the current UK HE context:

> All students, from all backgrounds, with the ability and the desire to undertake HE, are supported to access, succeed in, and progress from HE.
>
> (OfS, 2020)

One area of particular concern in UK HE at the moment is ***attainment gaps*** that have been highlighted by recent analyses. This is where gaps are identified between the achievements of some students compared to others. In particular, data has shown that black, Asian and minority ethnic (BAME) UK students are less likely to gain the best degree classifications compared to white UK students even though they have the same entry qualifications. Understandably, this is causing real concern, and institutions are currently devoting a lot of effort into understanding the reasons for this and trying to remove any barriers.

In terms of TNE, the diversity of the student population will vary depending on the context and the nature of provision, as will local policies on equality issues. Whilst the widening-participation targets and monitoring within the UK do not usually extend to TNE, they may influence the approach taken by your institution. In contrast, much of the expansion in TNE has been primarily focused on income generation and targeting students who can afford to pay more to gain a UK degree. So, there are tensions between the widening-participation approach within the UK and the expansion and marketing of UK HE overseas.

ONLINE AND BLENDED LEARNING

Advances in technology are changing the way in which HEIs operate, and this applies as much to teaching and learning as other areas.

KEY FEATURES OF UK HIGHER EDUCATION

Various terms are used to describe the use of technology for learning, such as *online learning*, *digital learning* and *blended learning*, where there is a mix of face-to-face and online learning. Most HEIs use some form of VLE for teaching and learning. Typically, there is a site for each module or unit on a course where relevant documents and teaching materials are shared with students, online activities are managed and communication forums hosted. The extent to which these are used often depends on the skills and enthusiasm of the teacher and the readiness of students to engage. As a result, some HEIs specify the minimum expected of staff in terms of these VLE sites. At the time of writing, the Covid-19 pandemic has forced HEIs across the globe to close and to transfer to online teaching within a very short period of time. Whilst this has been very stressful for staff and students, there are likely to be some benefits in terms of what they have learned from this experience and can be carried forward.

Many HEIs in the UK have been involved in the development of Massive Online Open Courses (MOOCs) on a whole range of subjects. These are university-level courses which are made available without having to enrol on a formal course, and are often free. Most of these are hosted on a platform called Future Learn where you can find more information about what is available (see *Further resources*).

SUMMARY

In this chapter, we have given you an insight into the scale of UK HE both within the UK and in TNE. We have looked at how UK HE is regulated, funded and quality-assured, and highlighted that policy and practice can vary across the four countries of the UK. We have highlighted some of the key issues currently affecting UK HE; i.e. teaching qualifications; competition for students; equality, diversity and inclusion; and online learning.

 FURTHER RESOURCES

Data

Discover Uni – official website for information on HE courses
www.discoveruni.gov.uk/

Higher Education Statistics Agency (HESA) – collects and publishes detailed information about UK HE
www.hesa.ac.uk/

KEY FEATURES OF UK HIGHER EDUCATION

Equality, diversity and inclusion

Butcher, C., Davies, C., and Highton, M. 2020. Designing Learning: From Module Outline to Effective Teaching. Abingdon: Routledge. Chapter 7, Learning Materials and Resources for Diverse Learners

Equality Act 2010 (Great Britain)
www.legislation.gov.uk/ukpga/2010/15/contents

Equality Commission for Northern Ireland
www.equalityni.org/Home

Equality, Diversity and Inclusion section of Advance HE website
www.advance-he.ac.uk/guidance/equality-diversity-and-inclusion

League tables

The Complete University Guide
www.thecompleteuniversityguide.co.uk/league-tables/rankings

The *Guardian* University Guide
www.theguardian.com/education/ng-interactive/2019/jun/07/university-league-tables-2020

The *Times* and *Sunday Times* Good University Guide
www.thetimes.co.uk/article/good-university-guide-in-full-tp6dzs7wn

Online learning

Future Learn MOOCs
www.futurelearn.com/

Quality assurance and enhancement

Advance HE – advisory body on HE
www.advance-he.ac.uk/

The Frameworks for Higher Education Qualifications of UK Degree-Awarding Bodies
www.qaa.ac.uk/quality-code/qualifications-and-credit-frameworks

Quality Assurance Agency
www.qaa.ac.uk/

Subject Benchmark Statements
www.qaa.ac.uk/quality-code/subject-benchmark-statements

Teaching Excellence and Student Outcomes Framework (TEF) – an exercise to assess excellence in teaching and student outcomes over and above the national standards
www.officeforstudents.org.uk/advice-and-guidance/teaching/what-is-the-tef/

KEY FEATURES OF UK HIGHER EDUCATION

UK Professional Standards Framework – national framework for teaching and learning in HE hosted on the Advance HE website
www.advance-he.ac.uk/guidance/teaching-and-learning/ukpsf

Rankings

QS World University Rankings (2020)
www.qs.com/rankings/

Times Higher Education (2020) World University Rankings
www.timeshighereducation.com/world-university-rankings

Regulation and funding

Department for the Economy (Northern Ireland)
www.economy-ni.gov.uk/

Higher Education Funding Council for Wales (HEFCW)
www.hefcw.ac.uk/

Office for Students (England)
www.officeforstudents.org.uk/

Scottish Funding Council
www.sfc.ac.uk/

Student surveys

The National Student Survey (NSS) – an annual survey of final-year undergraduates www.thestudentsurvey.com/

Student Barometer – a student survey available internationally
www.i-graduate.org/services/student-barometer/

UK transnational education

British Council website
www.britishcouncil.org/education/ihe/knowledge-centre/transnational-education

JISC TNE projects website
www.jisc.ac.uk/rd/projects/transnational-education

Universities UK international website on TNE
www.universitiesuk.ac.uk/International/Pages/tne.aspx

Chapter 2

Education in the UK

[UKPSF: V4]

KEY FINDINGS FROM OUR SURVEY

The main challenges respondents faced were:

- Not being familiar with the education system in the UK
- Assumptions being made about what they did know about the UK system
- Lack of training or induction about the UK education system.

These issues were clearly highlighted by a number of respondents. For example:

> It was hard to know the level of knowledge of students, the type of topics that the students worked on and how they learned to approach problems during their school and undergrad education as I am not used to the UK system.
> German researcher teaching in UK

> Teaching to students with UK education system background – I am not very familiar with their background knowledge and skills.
> Hungarian lecturer teaching in UK

> Not having knowledge of the educational system in UK for students in secondary school.
> American PhD student teaching in UK

> Being unaware of how UK education system works.
>
> Australian lecturer teaching in UK

> There are many things about higher education in the UK that I didn't know about (and didn't know I didn't know until I was in the middle of things). This includes everything from the academic calendar to what the procedures are for ... marking.
>
> American researcher teaching in the UK

Their advice was clear:

> Get an idea, how much the UK differs from the school/University system that you went through to avoid wrong assumptions when designing and delivering lectures and exams.
>
> German researcher teaching in the UK

> First few months should be spent understanding how the system works.
>
> Malaysian lecturer teaching in Malaysia

> Ask colleagues who are familiar with the UK system and understand the struggles of coming from another country.
>
> Italian lecturer teaching in the UK

Many respondents felt that a better induction and training on these aspects was needed, so we hope this chapter will, at least partly, address that issue for you.

INTRODUCTION

In Chapter 1, we covered the key features of UK higher education (HE) that we feel are essential for all those teaching in UK HE to understand. The aim of this chapter is to provide further background information about the education system in the UK, and you may find some sections more useful than others depending on your role and where you teach. If you teach in the UK, the *Pre-university education and qualifications* section will help you understand the educational background of your UK students and might also be of interest if you have children of school age. If you teach in transnational education (TNE), the sub-section *Post-compulsory education* will help you understand how the design of HE degrees builds on the earlier stages of education in the UK. The *Higher education* section builds on Chapter 1 and provides further information to help you understand aspects such as the history and nature of your institution, how students access and support themselves through HE and the academic calendar, so the relevance of this will vary depending on your role.

PRE-UNIVERSITY EDUCATION AND QUALIFICATIONS

Introduction

Education in the UK is divided into primary, secondary, further and higher education, and this section of the chapter will focus on the first three on that list. We are doing this as we thought it would be useful to try to give you an idea of the educational background of the students in your classes and courses, as it is most likely to be somewhat different to your experience and/or the situation in your own country. The problem is that it would take most of this book to give you the full details (and that is not the main point of the text), so we will give an outline and attempt to provide you with basic information about the:

- Way education is organised up to the age of 18 in the UK
- Sorts of qualifications your students will have (and how to find more about them)
- Types of educational experiences that your students will be bringing to your classes; which will, of course, set their expectations of you.

As we noted in Chapter 1, the UK consists of four countries. Scotland, Wales and Northern Ireland have their own devolved governments (with homes in their respective capitals), each with varying powers; but this power is delegated by the Parliament of the United Kingdom based in England. This is important, as you will find that the devolved powers impact considerably on the organisation of schools, the curriculum and pre-university examinations.

Types of school and who funds them

In 2018/19 there were 32,770 schools in the UK attended by just over nine million children. Of these:

- 3,714 were nurseries or early-learning centres – pre-school age group

- 20,832 were primary schools – typically catering for ages 4/5 to 11 – in some areas primary education is split into infant and junior schools
- 19 were middle schools – typically catering for ages 10 to 14
- 4,188 were secondary schools – typically catering for ages 11 to 16 or 11 to 18.

Of course, schools vary in size, and currently the smallest is Milburn Primary School with just six pupils whilst the largest secondary schools have over 2,500 pupils. Adding to the numbers, in 2018/19 there were:

- 2,408 independent schools
- 1,257 special schools (see *Further resources*)
- 352 pupil referral units (PRUs – see *Further resources*)
- 381 further education (FE) colleges, of which 94 were sixth-form colleges.

The above numbers give an indication of scale, but numbers are less important than the types of school mentioned, and we will come back to those below. Also, we have used *sixth form*, which is so named as it comes after five years of secondary school; pupils in the sixth form can be in an 11 to 18 school (where 11 to 16 are the first five years or forms) or in a sixth-form college. It is worth noting at this stage that the source of funding is important in deciding the type of school; basically, there are three major sources of funding for schools:

1. State-funded schools, when the money comes from the national government
2. State-funded schools, when the money comes from the local government (the local government is usually called the *local authority*). A local authority is an organisation that is officially responsible for all the public services and facilities in a particular area and gets money to do this from the national government and local taxes (e.g. council tax and local business tax)
3. Fees, paid by parents/guardians or from a scholarship or bursary.

By law, all children in the UK of compulsory school age (ages 5 to 16) must receive a full-time education that is suited to their age, ability, aptitude and special educational needs (SEN – hence the need for special schools mentioned in the list above). More than 90% of pupils attend publicly funded (national or local government) *state* schools and the remainder either attend a fee-paying, *independent* or *private* school or are home-schooled. Most teaching and learning in state schools in the UK is underpinned by the **National Curriculum** (see below for more details).

State schools receive funding from one of two sources: their local authority (local government) or directly from the national government. You will find that local to where you live and work there will be a range of different types of school at both primary and secondary level, and the most common types are:

- *Community schools*, which are also known as *local-authority-maintained schools*; they have no affiliation to business or any religion and must deliver the National Curriculum (funding = local authority).
- *Foundation schools* and *voluntary schools* – whilst these are also funded by the local authority, they enjoy more freedom over the way they organise themselves but must deliver the National Curriculum. In addition, they may have links to particular religious groups (funding = local authority).
- *Academies* and *free schools* are not tied to a local authority and are run by not-for-profit trusts. Academies and free schools do not have to follow the National Curriculum but do have to teach a "broad and balanced curriculum, including English, mathematics, science and religious education" (www.gov.uk/national-curriculum, n.d.). They have more freedom to organise how they run things (funding = national government).
- *City technology colleges* are independent of their local authority, located typically in urban areas and funded by central government, but industry/companies can also contribute. They emphasise teaching science and technology (funding = national government +).
- *Grammar schools*, which can be run by the local authority, a foundation body or an academy trust, so their source of funding can vary, and that decides the freedoms that they have. What makes them special is that they select their pupils based on academic ability and have entrance examinations or tests (funding = various).

Those schools that are not funded by the state but are financed by tuition fees, gifts and endowments are called private or independent schools (the terms are used interchangeably). The most exclusive (and expensive) private schools are referred to as *public schools* and these are mainly boarding; the pupils live at the school on a weekly or termly basis. Private schools can' set their own entrance requirements as long as they do not break UK laws against any form of discrimination. The ability to pay is an obvious hurdle to entrance but many private schools offer scholarships to attract poor but gifted pupils and provide means-tested bursaries. Some parents will make considerable sacrifices to send their children to private schools as the education offered, not prescribed by the National Curriculum, often results in high academic standards; which is often attributed to lower pupil–teacher ratios than found in state schools, more individual teaching and a greater emphasis on the development of personal attributes and abilities. Private schools usually offer a wide range of sporting, musical and artistic facilities, and pupils often gain cultural, social and professional advantages as a result of the ethos and social mix of the schools.

So far, we have covered the majority of school types that exist in the UK but have not said anything about FE, and we will return to that later. We have mentioned the National Curriculum several times, so we will look at that next as it covers schooling from about 5 to 16 and includes the first national qualifications that you need to know about and take into account.

The National Curriculum

The notion of a national curriculum sounds ideal, but life is not so simple. The first National Curriculum in the UK was introduced in 1988 (in England and Wales) but since that time the curriculum has evolved in different ways in each of the four countries in the UK. The National Curriculum is a set of subjects and standards used by primary and secondary schools in order that children study the same things. It covers what subjects are taught and the standards (attainment targets) children should reach in each subject at different ages. We will give a little more detail about the current National Curriculum in England as it introduces the concept of **key stages** linked to school years, pupil ages and assessment; see Table 2.1. In *Further resources* we have given links to the pre-university curricular in all four countries if you need more details or country-specific information.

The important points to note:

- KS1 and KS2 are the primary phase (KS1 = infant and KS2 = junior).
- At the end of KS2 there are national attainment tests and assessments.
- The break at KS2 to KS3 is the typical move from primary to secondary school.

EDUCATION IN THE UK

TABLE 2.1 The National Curriculum in England

Key stage	Year	Age	Assessment (in 2020)
KS1	1	5–6	Phonics screening check
	2	6–7	National tests and teacher assessments in English, maths and science
KS2	3	7–8	
	4	8–9	
	5	9–10	
	6	10–11	National tests and teacher assessments in English and maths, and teacher assessments in science
KS3	7	11–12	
	8	12–13	
	9	13–14	
KS4	10	14–15	
	11	15–16	Most children take the General Certificate of Secondary Education (GCSE) or other national qualifications

(www.gov.uk/national-curriculum)

- At the end of KS4 most pupils take national examinations.
- We tend to use the year to describe the stage of education, year 6 and year 11 being the most significant in terms of testing.

The age of 16 is significant in all four UK countries as this signifies the end of **compulsory schooling**. At this stage most pupils take examinations; currently a version of GCSEs in England, Wales and Northern Ireland, and Nationals in Scotland. We will give a few more details about those as they are the precursor examinations – gateways – to the curriculum and national examinations that are used to decide university entrance.

General Certificate of Secondary Education

In England, Wales and Northern Ireland the typical examination taken at age 16 is the GCSE. Typically pupils will take eight or nine GCSEs across a range of subjects; up to this point the aim is not to specialise, but rather to provide a broad and inclusive education. In England GCSEs are currently graded 9 (highest) to 1 (lowest) with 4 being a *standard* pass and U being ungraded/unclassified. In Wales and Northern Ireland they are graded A* to G, with A* being the top grade. Ofqual (www.gov.uk/government/organisations/ofqual), the qualifications regulator in England, has produced guidance which helps explain the differences and similarities between GCSE qualifications in England, Wales and Northern Ireland if you need more detail. Examination boards are responsible for setting and marking GCSE examinations, and we have listed the major boards in *Further resources* and given their web addresses. If you need more information about GCSEs, in particular the content covered, see www.gov.uk/government/collections/gcse-subject-content.

We will take a moment to look at the situation in Scotland – you will have noticed above that Scotland differs from other UK systems – before we move on to look at the qualifications that most 18-year-olds (year 13) will take prior to entering university. In Scotland, pupils move to secondary education at the age of 12, and at age 16 they take exams called National 3, National 4 and National 5 qualifications. National 3 and 4 courses are not graded (candidates receive a pass or fail), whilst National 5 courses are graded A to D or No Award. Grades A–C would usually allow a learner to progress to the next stage of education.

The important points to remember about GCSEs/Nationals:

- They mark the end of compulsory schooling.
- Pupils study a range of subjects – a broader education.
- They are the hurdle allowing pupils to go on to more advanced studies ending in examinations that are used to decide university entrance.
- At this stage some pupils may give up studying mathematics, science(s) and/or English in order to specialise at Advanced Level, so their GCSE/National grade gives you an indication of their standard in those subjects when they arrive in your courses.

Post-compulsory education

As we said above, by law all children in the UK of compulsory school age (ages about 5 to 16) must receive a full-time education; this is often referred to as *compulsory schooling*. But what happens after 16, after (post) compulsory education? The choices are:

- Stay on at their school, or in another school, in the sixth form (years 12 and 13)
- Go to a college of FE, which includes sixth-form colleges
- Do an apprenticeship (see *Further resources* for more)
- Do a programme of training and work experience
- Go into work full-time
- Take a gap year – perhaps for travel, volunteering, gaining work experience or earning money to pay HE fees.

Expectation across the UK varies, but in England all young people are now expected to stay in some kind of education, training or apprenticeship until they are 18, and this can be combined with 20 hours or more a week working or volunteering.

Those in *post-compulsory*, full-time education (typically in sixth forms or FE colleges) will be studying to take Advanced Level (A Level) examinations or Technical Level (T Level – from 2020/2021) or Highers in Scotland. Those who go to FE colleges can opt for a range of qualifications; some academic and others more professionally, technically or practically based. (See *Post-compulsory, full-time education* in *Further resources* for more details.) We will give more details about A Levels, T Levels and Highers as these are the usual qualifications that are used to admit students into university.

A Levels – Advanced Level qualifications

A Levels are subject-based qualifications, usually taken over two years, that can lead to university, further study, training or work. Pupils normally study three or four A Levels at the same time in their first year of sixth form, and most cut back to three in their second year. This is because university offers are normally based on three A Levels. They are usually assessed by unseen examinations, as the trend at the moment is away from course-work assessment (but this could change again). Normally, to take A Levels a pupil will need:

- At least five GCSEs at grades 9 to 4 (England) or A* to C (Wales/Northern Ireland)
- At least grade 6/5 or B/C in the specific subject(s) he or she wants to study.

However, the specific requirements needed to study A Levels will vary across schools and colleges.

In Chapter 1 we talked about the Framework for Higher Education Qualifications in England, Wales and Northern Ireland (FHEQ; see Table 1.2), and Level 4 was the lowest level for university-based qualifications. A Levels are Level 3 qualifications, the same as the International Baccalaureate (IB; see below). Pupils normally pick their courses based on the degree they wish to pursue at university; most degrees require specific A Level subjects for entry. A number of countries (including Singapore, Uganda, Kenya, Mauritius and Zimbabwe) have developed qualifications with the same name as, and a similar format to, A Levels.

T Levels – Technical Level qualifications

From 2020/2021 T Levels will be available and will be equivalent to three A Levels. These two-year courses are being developed in collaboration with employers and businesses so that they meet the needs of industry and commerce and prepare students for work. They will, however, have a **Universities and Colleges Admission Service** (UCAS) tariff (**UCAS tariff**), and this means that some of your students may have studied in this way.

A T Level is split into three main sections:

1. Technical Qualification (TQ) – the main, classroom-based element
2. Industry Placement – runs for a minimum of 45 days overall
3. Development in English, maths and digital literacy – built into the classroom-based element.

See T Levels *in Further resources* for more.

Highers (Scotland)

In Scotland, at the age of 16 pupils take exams called Nationals (see above) and then move on to Highers and Advanced Highers. Highers are the standard Scottish qualification for pupils planning to apply to university. They are usually taken, over one year, between the ages of 16 and 18, and most pupils take five different Highers. In the following year, the pupils can:

- Take Advanced Highers in subjects they are particularly good at or interested in, or which are key to their choice of course at university

- Upgrade or re-take Highers if they failed to achieve the grade needed
- Gain other skills and experience – for example, volunteering.

Most pupils complete this year as it improves the chances of getting on the course they want to do next, and an Advanced Higher qualification is essentially a simulation of the first year of university in that particular subject; this is the reason that Advanced Highers can be used for second-year university entry.

Baccalaureate

You may be aware of the IB, for which pupils study six subjects in their final two years, which must include English (or their own language in other countries), a second language, maths, a science and a humanities subject. Three of the subjects are studied and examined at a higher level (highers) than the other three (standards), but all are examined only at the end of the two years. In addition, pupils have to write a dissertation, sit a paper on theories of knowledge and complete more than 60 hours of after-school community service. It is reckoned to be equivalent to three A Levels. See *Further resources* for more about UK baccalaureates.

We have talked above about the types of schools that pupils can attend at both compulsory schooling (ages 5 to 16) and post-compulsory (ages 17 to 18). The alternative to staying on in the sixth form in a school is to go to college; i.e. go into FE.

Further education

FE includes any study after compulsory education that is not taken as part of an undergraduate or graduate degree (so pre-university level). Courses range from basic English and maths to City and Guilds, Foundation Degrees and Higher National Diplomas (HNDs). FE institutions include sixth-form colleges and colleges of FE. Whilst A Levels and Highers are the most widely accepted UK qualifications for entry to a university, there are many other relevant, FE qualifications which count towards entry that can be taken in FE; these include BTEC (British and Technology Education Council) Nationals, Higher National Certificates (HNCs) and HNDs.

BTEC Nationals

BTEC Nationals are awarded at three levels: Award, Certificate and Diploma. They all focus on particular vocational sectors, such as e-business, engineering, art and design, media, performing arts, agriculture, and health and social care. The BTEC Award is considered equivalent to one A Level, the Certificate to two A Levels and the Diploma to three A Levels. All provide a foundation for HE courses in the same subject area. They are rated as Level 3 qualifications on the FHEQ.

Higher National Certificates

These are considered a Level 4 qualification on the FHEQ (see Table 1.2 and *Further resources*: *What qualification levels mean*). They are available in many areas, including engineering, sports studies, art and design, media and communications, and music technology. Successful completion allows students to *top-up* to a degree by transferring into the second year of an appropriate degree course. They are primarily vocational qualifications and so also an excellent route into a variety of work in a range of industries and vocations, from electrical engineering to social care. Studying an HNC usually takes one year to complete full-time.

Higher National Diplomas

These are considered a Level 5 qualification on the FHEQ. They build on the subjects that can be studied at HNC, and successful completion allows students to *top-up* to a degree by transferring into the third year of an appropriate degree course. As with HNCs, they are primarily vocational qualifications and so an excellent route into a variety of work, and studying an HND usually takes one year to complete full-time.

Finally

As we said at the outset of this section on pre-university education and qualifications, we aimed to give you:

- A flavour and understanding of the types of schools and colleges that your students will have attended during their schooling and education from age 5 to 18

- An overview of the qualifications that they will have taken in order to gain their university place, and an idea of their educational experiences which may impact on their expectation of HE.

We have to add an important rider at this stage – pre-university education and qualifications are fluid and prone to change (just ask any school teacher!). We say this as the details may change after the publication of this text, but we trust that you will be able to use the content and resources included to gain an updated version.

HIGHER EDUCATION

HE includes any study after compulsory education that leads to the awarding of a degree. The various qualifications were outlined in Chapter 1 in the *Quality assurance* section. In Chapter 1 we also discussed the scale of UK HE and TNE and the key features of UK HE, so if you have not already read that chapter we would strongly recommend you do so. In this section, we aim to provide further information about three aspects of UK HE which we think will help you understand the context. First, we will give a brief history of UK HE to help you appreciate where some of the current policies and practices come from and how the different types of universities have emerged. We shall then focus on students and how they gain a place at university and fund themselves, and their expectations. Finally, we shall take a look at a typical academic calendar for UK HE.

A brief history of higher education in the UK

HE in the UK has a long history, with the University of Oxford and University of Cambridge (both in England) dating back to the eleventh and thirteenth centuries respectively, placing them among the oldest universities in the world. The first university colleges in Scotland were established in the fifteenth century (St Andrews, Glasgow, Aberdeen and Edinburgh) and together these universities are often referred to as the *ancient universities*. The first university colleges in Wales (University of Wales, Lampeter) and Northern Ireland (Queen's University Belfast) were established in the nineteenth century. At the same time, a major expansion of HE led to many medical and engineering colleges gaining university status. These universities, established up until 1963, are often called *civic* or *redbrick universities* and tend to focus more on real-world subjects of science, technology, medicine and engineering compared to the traditional focus on divinity and liberal arts.

In the last century, there have been two main periods of expansion in UK HE. During the 1960s a number of new universities opened across the UK. At the same time, a government review of HE recommended an expansion in HE and resulted in major changes to how post-school education was organised (see Chapter 1 regarding student numbers). The **Robbins Report** (Robbins, 1963) recommended that all colleges of advanced technology (in England and Wales) should be given university status and local colleges and technical institutions in England, Wales and Northern Ireland should become *polytechnics*. The universities established between 1963 and 1992 are described as *plate-glass universities*. The Robbins Report also recommended that university places should be available to all those who had the ability, and this became known as the *Robbins principle*. As a result, free tuition and maintenance grants were introduced for students.

The Further and Higher Education Act in 1992 made changes to the administration and funding of HE in England and Wales. It gave degree-awarding powers to the polytechnics and colleges of HE, enabling them to become universities and in so doing abolished the two-tier system of HE and brought together the liberal and vocational forms of education. These former polytechnics are often referred to as *new universities* or *post-1992 universities*, whereas those that were established before are referred to as *old* or *traditional universities*. In terms of funding, separate funding councils were set up in England, Scotland, Wales and Northern Ireland.

Later that decade, the UK government commissioned another major review of HE in the UK by Lord Dearing, resulting in a series of reports (Dearing, 1997). The **Dearing Report** made 93 recommendations about the expansion, funding and maintenance of standards in HE. One of the most significant was the recommendation that there should be tuition fees for HE. As a result, tuition fees were introduced across the UK in 1998, with students paying £1,000 per year up-front. The nature of fees has changed over the years and is different in each of the four countries (see Chapter 1). Another relevant recommendation in the context of this book was the introduction of training for teaching staff on how to teach. This has led to most universities having compulsory training courses for new academics and optional or compulsory training for researchers and PhD students who teach (see chapters 1 and 8). Finally, the report recommended the expansion of sub-degree and degree-level courses, arguing that there was sufficient demand from employers for applicants with higher qualifications. Soon afterwards, in 1999 the Labour government announced a target of 50% of young adults going into HE by 2010, but this target was not reached until 2017/18.

When universities were publicly funded there was a cap on the number of students they could recruit. If they exceeded this number, they did not get any funding for the additional students. As the funding shifted from public funds to individual students, these caps were gradually relaxed until they were abolished in England in 2015/16, allowing universities to recruit as many students as they wanted and increasing the competition for students between HE institutions. A cap on student numbers remains in Scotland due to there being no tuition fees.

Types of universities

As explained above, universities in the UK are often described in terms of when they gained university status. However, there are also groups of universities that have formed an alliance around shared missions and characteristics, and these group names are also used to describe universities.

- Russell Group Universities – a group of 24 universities who share a strong commitment to world-class research, education and contribution to society. It includes many of the oldest universities. The group formed at a meeting in Russell Road in London in 1994, hence the name.
- University Alliance – a group of 24 technical and professional universities with an emphasis on linking learning and practical experience through applied research and practical skills-based learning.
- MillionPlus Group – a group of 22 universities that claim to be the voice of twenty-first-century HE and are committed to facing global economic, social and cultural challenges.
- GuildHE – a group of about 50 smaller universities, FE colleges, professional bodies and specialist institutions that specialise in art, design, music, performance arts, agriculture and other specialist subjects.
- Cathedrals Group – a group of 15 universities and colleges that unite on ethical and faith grounds and have a strong commitment to social justice.

Knowing the history of your institution and whether it belongs to any of these groups can help you understand the whole approach and philosophy underpinning the institution. To find out which group your university belongs to, please see the website links for each group in *Further resources*.

Students

Gaining a place at university

The vast majority of applications for full-time undergraduate courses in the UK (home and international students) are handled by a central application service called the Universities and Colleges Admission Service. The exception to this is Scotland, where one-third of undergraduate courses are in FE colleges which are not covered by UCAS. Hence UCAS data for Scotland only covers two-thirds of undergraduate provision in Scotland. When applying through UCAS, undergraduate applicants can select up to five courses, but there are some restrictions, such as a limit of four courses for certain subjects (medicine, etc.) and only one course at either the University of Oxford or University of Cambridge. Further information can be found on the UCAS website (see *Further resources*).

There is no central service for postgraduate course applications, so this is done either by direct application to the institution or, for a small number of institutions, via the UCAS postgraduate service. This effectively means that applications to postgraduate courses are unlimited. However, it can be very time-consuming as each institution has its own application process!

There are a whole range of comparison websites which have appeared and aim to help students choose where and what they want to study. Discover Uni (see *Further resources*) is the official website for information and guidance on HE in the UK and is jointly owned by the regulatory bodies in the four countries of the UK. The site aims to help students decide whether HE is for them and to provide information and data about undergraduate courses in the UK. There are many other commercial websites that aim to help UK and international students decide where to study (see *Further resources*).

In terms of TNE, the application process may vary depending on the nature of the provision and the regulations within the overseas country, so find out how students apply at your institution.

Maintenance grants and loans

At the same time as student fees increased for UK students, maintenance grants have been reduced and for the most part replaced by loans which generally depend on household income. Again the approaches differ in the four countries of the UK but are generally a mix of a grant (bursary in

Scotland) and a loan that is repaid after the student starts earning over a certain threshold. As a result this is often described as a graduate tax.

Student expectations

The increase in HE fees in most parts of the UK has definitely had an influence on student expectations of their HE experience:

> Our students are more discerning; conscious of their personal investment in, and the value of, their studies; and outcome-orientated. They are increasingly consumer-minded and expect a modern, technologically adept learning environment that matches shifting lifestyles.
>
> (Scottish Funding Council, 2019, p.9)

Given the fees they are paying, many students have greater expectations in terms of the accommodation, facilities and resources available for them, and it is understandable that they expect value for money. As a result, *students as customers* has been used by some; however, this raises issues around the customer always being right and the notion of students buying an education or even a degree. Unfortunately, the plethora of league tables, student surveys and performance measures discussed in Chapter 1 can inflate the *students as customers* notion.

An alternative metaphor that has been used to describe university is a gym membership. Tuition fees give students access to the *gym* and expert tuition but if they don't exercise then they won't get fit. This is probably better than students as customers but still has issues, not least because of the high dropout rates from gyms! The key thing to stress with students is that they need to be active participants in their own education; it is not something they can just be given. In recent years, there has been a growing emphasis on engaging students at all levels of decision making at HE institutions and viewing them as partners and co-producers of knowledge rather than consumers of it.

The academic calendar

One of the things that new international staff often find confusing about UK HE is the structure of the academic year and **terms** and **semesters**. Traditionally, the academic year at university was divided into three terms of 8–12 weeks with Term 1 typically being from September/October until before Christmas (25 December), Term 2 being from January to before Easter (sometime around March/April) and Term 3 being from

Terms

Sep	Oct	Nov	Dec	Jan	Feb	Mar	April	May	June	July	Aug
S	Term 1		C		Term 2		E	Term 3		S	
S	Teaching		C		Teaching		E	Teach	Exam	S	

Semesters

Sep	Oct	Nov	Dec	Jan	Feb	Mar	April	May	June	July	Aug
S	Semester 1				Semester 2					S	
S	Teaching		C	Exam	Teaching		E	Teach	Exam	S	

C – Christmas (25 Dec) and New Year (1 Jan) holiday break
E – Easter holiday break. The date of Easter changes each year.
S – Summer holidays

FIGURE 2.1 Term and semester dates example

Easter until June. However, since the early 1990s an increasing number of institutions have moved to dividing the academic year into two semesters. *Semester* literally means "six months" but is effectively used in HE to divide the academic year into two halves, usually with exams at the end of each semester. So the first semester typically starts around September/October and runs until January, and the second starts around February and ends in June. Some universities, such as the University of Oxford and University of Cambridge, still follow the traditional three-term structure but the majority of institutions now use the semester structure. However, the Christmas and Easter holiday periods in the UK fall within the semester blocks and hence both semester and term dates are usually published to show how the year is divided academically (semesters) and how it is divided practically (around holidays). See Figure 2.1 for an example.

So, most students in the UK have a 3-month break over the summer months. However, a number of universities have now introduced a 2-year degree by adding an extra term over the summer period so students can complete their degree in 2 years as opposed to 3.

The introduction of semesters was part of a wider redesign of the curriculum in the early 1990s called **modularisation**. This came about when student numbers had expanded and there was a growing interest in giving students more choice and flexibility in terms of what they studied. With modularisation, courses are divided into chunks (modules or units) and these are taught within and assessed at the end of each semester. Students have more choice as to which modules they take, although it is usual for there to be core or required modules to gain a certain degree qualification.

For those involved in UK TNE, it is likely that holiday dates will be more aligned with local national holidays and, depending on how these fall, *terms* may not be used at all, so find out how the academic calendar works at your location. It is also useful to be aware of the UK academic calendar for your institution as that can impact on various aspects of your work; e.g. most universities close completely between Christmas and New Year, so you are unlikely to get responses to any emails sent during that period, and you also need to know when exam boards take place at the UK institution.

SUMMARY

In this chapter we aimed to provide you with additional background information on the UK education system to help you understand how UK students have been educated and how HE builds on the previous stages of education in the UK.

 FURTHER RESOURCES

Pre-university education and qualifications

Examination boards

Schools and colleges are free to select boards on a subject-by-subject basis. Currently, there are eight major exam boards available to schools offering a range of GCSEs, A Levels, T Levels, Highers, etc.:

- Assessment and Qualifications Alliance (AQA)
  www.aqa.org.uk
- City & Guilds
  www.cityandguilds.com
- Council for the Curriculum, Examinations & Assessment (CCEA)
  www.ccea.org.uk
- Oxford, Cambridge and RSA Examinations (OCR)
  www.ocr.org.uk
- Pearson/Edexcel
  https://qualifications.pearson.com/en/home.html
- Scottish Qualifications Authority (SQA)
  www.sqa.org.uk
- University of Cambridge International Examinations (CIE)
  www.cambridgeinternational.org
- Welsh Joint Education Committee (WJEC)
  www.wjec.co.uk

EDUCATION IN THE UK

National curricula in the four UK countries

England
www.gov.uk/government/collections/national-curriculum

Northern Ireland
www.nidirect.gov.uk/articles/school-curriculum

Scotland – Curriculum for Excellence (CfE)
www.gov.scot/policies/schools/school-curriculum/

Wales
www.hwb.gov.wales/curriculum-for-wales

Post-compulsory education

Apprenticeship

www.gov.uk/topic/further-education-skills/apprenticeships

Baccalaureate

English Baccalaureate (EBacc)
www.gov.uk/government/publications/english-baccalaureate-ebacc/english-baccalaureate-ebacc

International Baccalaureate (IB)
www.ibo.org

Scottish Baccalaureates
www.sqa.org.uk/sqa/34638.9432.html

Welsh Baccalaureate
www.wjec.co.uk/en/qualifications/welsh-baccalaureate-national-foundation#tab_overview

Post-compulsory, full-time education

www.ucas.com/further-education/post-16-qualifications/post-16-qualifications-you-can-take

T Levels

www.tlevels.gov.uk

www.gov.uk/government/publications/introduction-of-t-levels/introduction-of-t-levels

EDUCATION IN THE UK

Pupil referral unit (PRU)

PRUs cater for children who cannot attend a mainstream school, and pupils are often referred to one if they need specialist care and support above that a standard school can provide. For more details, see: www.theschoolrun.com/what-is-a-pupil-referral-unit

Special schools in the UK

Special schools are those that provide an education for children with a special educational need or disability. For more details and guidance, see:

www.specialneedsuk.org

www.theschoolrun.com/what-is-a-special-school

www.gov.uk/types-of-school

What qualification levels mean

The Frameworks for Higher Education Qualifications of UK Degree-Awarding Bodies
www.qaa.ac.uk/quality-code/qualifications-and-credit-frameworks

UK Government guidance
www.gov.uk/what-different-qualification-levels-mean/list-of-qualification-levels

Higher education

University groups

A guide to the different university groups
www.ukstudyoptions.com/uk-university-groups-a-quick-guide/

Comparison websites

The Complete University Guide
www.thecompleteuniversityguide.co.uk/

Discover Uni
www.discoveruni.gov.uk/

Study in UK – Guide for international Students
www.studyin-uk.com/study-guide/

UK Education Guide
www.ukeducationguide.com/universities/

University Compare
www.universitycompare.com/

The Uni Guide
www.theuniguide.co.uk/

What Uni?
www.whatuni.com/

University mission groups

Cathedrals Group
www.cathedralsgroup.ac.uk

GuildHE Group
www.guildhe.ac.uk

MillionPlus Group
www.millionplus.ac.uk

Russell Group of universities
www.russellgroup.ac.uk

University Alliance Group
www.unialliance.ac.uk

Universities and Colleges Admissions Service (UCAS)

The UK HE application service for the majority of undergraduate and some postgraduate courses.
www.ucas.com/

Chapter 3

How students learn and what the implications are for teaching

[UKPSF: A5, K3 & V3]

INTRODUCTION

Students come to higher education (HE) for many reasons but ultimately they do so to learn a subject and gain a degree. What they learn will vary depending on the nature of the subject, the level of study (undergraduate or postgraduate) and where they are in their learning journey. In the UK, the subject benchmark statements (QAA, 2020) mentioned in Chapter 1 outline what graduates of each subject are expected to know, do and understand at the end of their degree. Whilst much of this will be subject-specific, there are some commonalities across the subjects in terms of generic attributes of a graduate. These often, but not exclusively, include critical thinking, problem solving, independent learning and communicating effectively. It has become increasingly common for universities to specify what it is their graduates will come out with; i.e. *graduate outcomes or attributes*. For an example, have a look at the University of Edinburgh Graduate Attributes Framework (see *Further resources*).

Once we are clear about what it is we want students to learn, we then need to consider how we help them learn. There are many theories and extensive research about learning that emanate from different academic disciplines, including education, psychology, sociology and neuroscience, and have influenced teaching practice over the years. They have been categorised in various ways, and a common categorisation used is that of Merriam et al. (2006):

- *Behaviourist theories* – learning is a change in behaviour and the use of stimuli (reward and punishment) can shape behaviour.

- *Cognitivist theories* – learning is a change in the internal structures of the brain and the focus is on how information is stored, retrieved and processed.
- *Constructivism theories* – learners construct their own understanding of what they are learning based on their previous knowledge and experiences, linked to cognitive and social theories.
- *Social and situational theories* – people learn from interacting with others and the environment.
- *Humanistic theories* – learning is about self-fulfilment and the focus is on the individual learner and helping them to achieve their potential.

(Adapted from Merriam et al., 2006)

Rather than there being one over-riding theory of learning, much of what we currently do in terms of teaching and learning has been influenced by elements of these different learning theories. It is beyond the scope of this text to explain and review each of these theories in depth; this information is available elsewhere (see *Further resources* for some suggestions). Instead, in this chapter, we shall take a fairly pragmatic approach and focus on aspects that are currently influencing teaching and learning in UK HE. In reading this chapter, it is important for you to consider how the ideas and practices discussed resonate with or differ from your own experiences of HE as this can vary considerably in different countries.

INFLUENCES ON UK HE

The research on teaching and learning in HE that has influenced the UK has emerged from Europe (in particular, the UK and Scandinavia) and Australia over the last 30–40 years. This research takes a **student-centred approach** – i.e. it focuses on the students and how they learn, rather than on the teacher and what they do (a **teacher-centred approach**). It also proposes that knowledge is not just transferred to students, and therefore we need to focus on how students learn rather than just what they should learn and what we, as teachers, should do. Two key elements of this research have been **constructivism** and a concept called **approaches to learning**, so we shall discuss these first.

Constructivism

This theory emerged from cognitive psychology and claims that learners construct their own understanding of what they are learning based on their previous knowledge and experiences. Learners are not empty vessels to be passively filled with knowledge by their teacher, but instead they are *actively* involved in the learning process, making sense of new information and ideas by connecting them to their previous knowledge and experience. Jean Piaget, a cognitive psychologist, argued that knowledge is held within cognitive structures called ***schema*** and that the learner tries to fit new information into existing schema (***assimilation***), but if the new information conflicts with existing knowledge the learner has to adapt the schema to the new information (***accommodation***) (Illeris, 2017). So, although a lecturer may present the same information to a group of students, each student will construct their own understanding (or misunderstanding) of what has been presented. Whilst passively receiving information from a lecturer is effective in terms of helping students remember and understand, there is growing evidence that active learning methods result in better outcomes in terms of student learning. Another branch of constructivism is social constructivism, which maintains that social interaction is a key part of the learning process. We shall discuss active learning methods and social constructivism further later in this chapter.

Approaches to learning

Research carried out in the 1970s showed that the approach a student takes to learning depends on what it is they are being asked to learn. Marton and Säljö (1976) identified two main approaches: a ***surface approach*** and a ***deep approach***. With a surface approach the intention of the learner is to memorise the information presented to them so they can reproduce it later. With a deep approach the intention of the learner is to try and understand the meaning. The defining features of the approaches were outlined by Entwistle (1997) and are presented in Table 3.1.

It is important to note that the approach to learning is not a fixed trait but a response to the context of learning. So the teacher can encourage a certain approach to learning by the design of learning activities and assessments. For instance, if the teacher sets a multiple-choice test for students on knowledge of facts and figures, this is likely to encourage a surface approach to learning where students memorise the information. If the teacher asks students to apply a theory to their practice and evaluate the effectiveness of that, this will encourage a deep approach to learning. However, as we will see, it is not as simple as that because other factors affect whether a student takes a deep or surface approach to learning. Ultimately, we want all our graduates to be able to take a deep approach to learning, but that does not mean that there is anything wrong with surface learning in itself; it just isn't sufficient.

TABLE 3.1 Defining features of deep and surface approaches to learning

Deep approach	
Intention	To understand ideas for yourself
By	Relating ideas to previous knowledge and experience
	Looking for patterns and underlying principles
	Checking evidence and relating it to conclusions
	Examining logic and argument cautiously and critically
	Becoming actively interested in the course content
Surface approach	
Intention	To cope with course requirements
By	Studying without reflecting on either purpose or strategy
	Treating the course as unrelated bits of knowledge
	Memorising facts and procedures routinely
	Finding difficulty in making sense of new ideas presented
	Feeling undue pressure and worry about work

(From Entwistle, 1997, p.19)

A constructivist view of learning and the approaches to learning research have had a major influence on teaching practices in UK. In the rest of this chapter, we shall focus on what we know about student learning and what the implications are for teaching, and we have divided these into three sections:

- What students bring
- Course context
- Environment.

In so doing, we shall make reference to some ideas and practices that have emerged from the different theories identified above, and build on the work of Butcher et al. (2020), who developed a list of 12 things that can help learning. We do not claim that what follows is a fully comprehensive list, but rather some of the key things we think will help give you an insight into teaching and learning in UK HE.

WHAT STUDENTS BRING

The common thread throughout this section is difference. Students come to university for different reasons and from a variety of backgrounds, and this means their starting points are all different, which affects many aspects of their learning. Students bring different beliefs, motivation, knowledge and abilities, and as teachers we should seek to understand and embrace these differences (see the *Equality, diversity and inclusion* section in Chapter 1).

1. Background

Students come from a wide range of backgrounds and with different personal circumstances, all of which can affect their confidence and readiness to learn. Whilst many students in the UK will be 18-year-old school leavers, there is an increased diversity of students in terms of socioeconomic background, education background, international students (including non-native English speakers) and students with disabilities (seen or hidden). All institutions should have a process in place to ensure that teachers know if they have any students with a disability in their class and what adjustments if any they require, but bear in mind that not all students choose to declare their disability. Most institutions now have some sort of analytics software to track various characteristics of students (and staff) and can provide useful information such as percentages of males v females, UK v international students, mature v young, different ethnic origin, educational background, etc.

Implications for teaching

Find out as much as you can about who your students are and what their support needs are; for example, are any of them carers, single parents, international students and non-native English speakers? Check how you will be notified if you are teaching a student that has declared a disability, and what their support needs are. Chapter 7 focuses on student support and the importance of induction and transition programmes to help students adjust to university.

2. Beliefs

Students come into HE with different beliefs about what knowledge is and what learning involves, and these can shape how they learn. A longitudinal study carried out in the United States (Perry, 1970) showed that students' understanding of what knowledge is develops as they progress through their university course. The beliefs change from seeing knowledge as either right or wrong (dualism) towards use of evidence to reach conclusions, and beyond that to accepting that knowledge is still developing (relativism). This shift from seeing knowledge as black and white to it being a grey area brings increasing levels of uncertainty, which the learner needs to be able to deal with.

Around the same time, Säljö (1979) identified five conceptions (beliefs) of learning and a later study, carried out in UK HE, by Marton et al. (1993) found similar categories but added a sixth, describing learning as:

- Increasing one's knowledge
- Memorising and reproducing
- Applying
- Understanding
- Seeing something in a different way
- Changing as a person.

Students' beliefs about knowledge and learning will be influenced by their prior learning experiences, such as school, and therefore they may see learning as fundamentally about memorising and reproducing information. Getting the results of their first assessment at university can be a shock for students when they realise that reproducing information in the same way as they have done at school may get them a pass but won't get them a high grade. If a student believes that learning is memorising and reproducing information then they are unlikely to adopt a deep approach even if the task set encourages such an approach, hence teachers may need to change students' beliefs about knowledge and learning.

> Students fresh from school often see learning in narrow reproductive terms, but going through higher education their conception broadens as they recognise the importance of developing their own understanding of course material.
>
> (Entwistle, 1997, p.17)

Implications for teaching

Teachers need to be aware that students may have very different beliefs about what knowledge is and what learning involves. The main way in which teachers can change student beliefs is through exposing them to different knowledge ideas, environments and teaching and learning activities that help develop their conceptions of knowledge and learning. To support students in their transition into HE, most universities have induction programmes and first-year modules that focus on helping students understand what learning means in the UK HE context. More information about this can be found in Chapter 7.

3. Motivation

In an ideal world, all our students would come to university with a passion for and intrinsic interest in the subject they have chosen to study. It is likely that students with this intrinsic motivation will have developed that over time, as their interest and success in the subject has grown. There are, however, many different reasons why people choose to study for a degree. Some students are extrinsically motivated by the desire to get a degree which leads to a certain job and can be a way out of poverty for some. It can be very frustrating for teachers when students are extrinsically motivated and only seem interested in what is on the exam rather than in learning the subject in itself, and some teachers feel it is the students' responsibility to motivate themselves, not theirs. However, instead of blaming students, teachers need to try and understand why motivation varies, act as a role model and share their passion and enthusiasm for their subject.

Abraham Maslow argued that people are motivated to realise their own potential – i.e. to self-actualise – but that they can only do this if their basic needs are satisfied first (Maslow, 1954). Maslow's human motivation theory is classed as a humanist theory of learning, and his *hierarchy of needs* is often depicted as a pyramid (see Figure 3.1). The first, lowest level is basic physiological needs (food, water, shelter), then safety needs, then a sense of belonging followed by self-esteem. Only when those needs have been satisfied can learners reach their full potential. The higher up the pyramid a learner is,

FIGURE 3.1 Maslow's hierarchy of needs

then the more motivated they will be to learn and the more effective their learning will be.

Implications for teaching

Teachers need to recognise that students come to university for different reasons and are motivated in different ways. Teachers sharing their passion and enthusiasm for their subject can help motivate learners. In the *Course context* section below we shall discuss some strategies teachers can use to help motivate students during their time at university.

4. Prior knowledge

A key aspect of a constructivist view of learning is that the learner comes with pre-existing knowledge and understanding; they are not empty vessels. Students come to university with different levels of knowledge, both about the subject they have chosen to study and more generally. Although each degree course normally has standard entry requirements, there are various types of qualifications with different syllabi (see Chapter 2) and the level of attainment and background in allied subjects will vary. Even if two students have studied the same A Level course and gained the same grade, what they know (or think they know) will be different as the way in which they have constructed their knowledge will differ.

An American psychologist David Ausubel once said:

> The most important single factor influencing learning is what the learner already knows. Ascertain this and teach him/her accordingly.
> (Ausubel, 1968, in Dennick, 2014, p.44)

Implications for teaching

Teachers need to find out what their students already know, challenge any misconceptions and build on their existing knowledge. Diagnostic tests, initial tasks and discussion can be good ways to establish current knowledge.

COURSE CONTEXT

In this section, we shall highlight some of the contextual factors that influence student learning, such as aspects of course design, teaching methods and assessment. Chapters 4–6 discuss these factors in detail, so here we just give an overview of how they affect student learning.

5. Clear learning outcomes

It might seem obvious but it is important that students know what it is they are meant to learn and how they will be assessed. Behaviourist psychologists in the 1950s (Bloom, 1956) advocated the use of learning objectives to set out what the teachers' objectives were and target outcomes. The Dearing report in 1997 (see Chapter 2) recommended that every degree programme develop a programme specification in which they specified what the outcomes of learning would be for students (Dearing, 1997). As a result the aims, *learning outcomes*, teaching and learning activities and assessments are specified for each degree programme and module in UK HE. Learning outcomes focus on what the student can do at the end of their learning. John Biggs introduced the term *constructive alignment*, which brings together a constructivist view of learning and the importance of aligning the learning outcomes, teaching and learning activities and assessment (Biggs, 1999). The importance of constructive alignment in curriculum design is explained in Chapter 4.

Implications for teaching

Be clear about what you want your students to learn. Ensure that your learning outcomes, teaching and learning activities and assessment align. Share and discuss learning outcomes with students.

6. Relevance

Earlier in this chapter, we discussed the fact that students have different motives for wanting to gain a degree. One way in which teachers can motivate students to learn is to help them see the relevance and value of what they are learning. As teachers in HE, we are usually passionate about our subject and have developed courses with a clear view of what we want our students to achieve. This informs the design of the curriculum, and as teachers we can clearly justify what we want our students to learn. However, we are not always very explicit about this with students and often they cannot see the relevance of what they are being taught, especially when your session is only one of many that week. Or they don't realise that it is the precursor to something that comes later that they do not know about yet. Thus it is important that we share that sort of information with our students so they understand why they need to learn what they are being taught.

Implications for teaching

Contextualise the learning at the start of a module or individual teaching session and explain how what students are learning fits into the bigger picture. Use case studies or examples from your own experience or link to commercial, industrial or economic examples to demonstrate real-world significance. Make connections between what students are currently learning and what they learned previously or will learn in the future. Help students make connections between different chunks of learning so they can construct their own understanding. Giving students choices about which modules they study or which topics to focus on for a particular task can also enhance their motivation. Many degree courses have a final-year project or dissertation module that allows students some choice over their focus. See Chapter 5 for further information.

7. Structure of content

According to Butcher et al. (2020), as the subject expert you "should be able to sequence the ideas, concepts and content in the most appropriate way to support students' learning" (p.86). To do this you need to identify the key concepts in your subject and help students develop their own conceptual map of the subject. One way of helping students to understand the content of a subject is through *threshold concepts* (Meyer and Land, 2003). These are the key concepts that a student needs to grasp to really understand a subject. They are often troublesome concepts that students struggle with, but when they grasp them it opens up a new way of thinking, transforming their understanding. Not all key concepts in a subject are considered threshold ones. A range of research has been published on threshold concepts in a variety of subjects so it is worth finding out what is known about your subject. See the useful text by Land et al. (2008) in *Further resources* for more information.

Another aspect related to content is whether students have preferences for how information is presented and how they prefer to learn. One of the most contested areas in terms of student learning research over the last 50 years has been around the concept of *learning styles*. Advocates believe that individual learners have a particular learning style that can be assessed and should influence the approach taken to learning by the learner and the approach to teaching by their teacher. However, there has been significant criticism of the inventories used to assess learning styles and there is no research evidence to support the notion that matching teaching style to learning style enhances learning. There does seem to be general agreement that learners may have preferences for how information is presented – e.g. visually, aurally – and how they prefer to learn. It is not practical to tailor teaching to each students' preferences, so instead the main focus should be on selecting the most appropriate way to present information for the particular content being taught. Some argue that we tend to teach the way we like to learn, so we should also consider presenting information in a variety of ways, when appropriate, to cater for all students' needs.

Implications for teaching

Identify the key concepts in your subject and provide an organised and sequenced pathway through them (Butcher et al., 2020). Try and identify what the threshold concepts are in your subject and how students have the opportunity to learn, be assessed and gain feedback on their understanding of these key concepts. Consider the prior knowledge, ability and interests of your students and decide how best to present information for the particular content you are teaching.

8. Experience

The idea that students learn through experience and reflecting on it, *experiential learning*, comes from the work of David Kolb, who developed the Experiential Learning Theory (Kolb, 1984). Kolb built on the work of other psychologists interested in the role of experience and developed a cycle of four stages: experience, reflection, contextualising and then planning. The learning process often begins with an experience, but learning can start at any stage. Kolb believed that, for learning to be effective, learners need to work through all four stages of the cycle. Whilst aspects of Kolb's cycle have been criticised, there has been growing interest in the role of experience in student learning. In particular, experiential learning has been very influential in professional courses such as medical education that have a significant amount of work-based learning. On many courses, students have opportunities such as work placements and field trips to gain experience and reflect on it to inform their thinking and future practice, and getting feedback on their experiences is a key aspect of the process. It is not always feasible or possible for students to get experience in a work setting or field trip, so instead these experiences can be replicated to some extent via practical and laboratory classes and through case- and problem-based learning. These teaching methods are discussed in Chapter 5.

Implications for teaching

According to Biggs and Tang (2011), what students do is more important than what we as teachers do. Give students the opportunity to learn by doing. Where feasible, incorporate placements, field trips and industrial visits into your course or use practical classes and case- and problem-based learning to replicate real-life situations. Encourage students to reflect on the experience and what they have learned.

9. Challenge

We mentioned social constructivism earlier, which emphasises the role of social interaction in individuals' developing their understanding. This theory was proposed in 1978 by a Russian psychologist, Lev Vygotsky, who believed that culture, language and social interaction drive learning, and emphasised the critical role of teachers in extending an individual learner's potential (Hunt and Chalmers, 2012). He argued that teachers could extend a learner's learning beyond their actual zone of development that they can attain independently to a *zone of proximal development* (see Figure 3.2). Teachers can do this through having contact and interaction with the learner and by using activities such as questions, demonstrations, peer discussions, analogies and group and individual tasks. *Scaffolding* was later introduced by Jerome Bruner and colleagues (Wood, Bruner and Ross, 1976) to describe the structured activities that teachers provide to extend the students learning. So the teacher's role is to provide the scaffolding to help extend the learners and, of course, differentiating between more capable students and those that need additional support is really important.

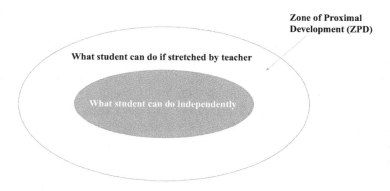

FIGURE 3.2 Vygotsky's zone of proximal development
(Figure based on Stewart, 2012)

The social interaction between students is also an important part of the learning process. Working collaboratively with peers can help scaffold an individual's learning. A group of students working together to solve a problem will often come up with solutions that each individual learner would not have been able to do on their own. As learners develop, they become less reliant on the teacher or others for support and become more independent learners, which is one of the main aims of HE.

Implications for teaching

Teachers play a key part in providing the scaffolding to extend their learners' learning. They can do this by setting tasks, problems and activities that challenge students and support them to be successful. Providing opportunities for students to work collaboratively is also important.

10. Assessment

We have talked about the importance of constructive alignment between learning outcomes, teaching and learning activities and assessment. According to Gibbs and Simpson (2005) assessment has "an overwhelming influence on what, how and how much students study" (p.3). They claim that assessment in HE has traditionally focused on measuring student learning, but instead they argue that in designing assessments the primary focus should be on supporting learning. To do this, teachers need to consider the volume of the assessment, the focus and the quality of learning. Careful design of assessments encourages students to devote sufficient time on tasks, helps focus them on the most important aspects of a course and engages them in productive learning. A common saying is *assessment drives learning*. So if you want to change what students do and how they are learning, change the assessment. See Chapter 6 for more advice on assessment.

Implications for teaching

Design assessments that encourage time on task, focus students on the most important aspects of the course and encourages quality learning.

11. Feedback

Feedback is a critical part of the learning process and has been shown in various meta-analyses to have one of the largest effects on learning. Students need to know how they are doing and what they need to do to improve, so constructive feedback can help enhance learning. The timing of the feedback is important in terms of students being able to use that feedback to enhance their learning. There is growing interest in the notion of feedback being a dialogue between teacher and learner rather than being something that teachers give learners. See Chapter 6 for more advice on feedback.

Implications for teaching

Ensure regular opportunities for students to receive and discuss specific and timely feedback that will help develop their understanding.

ENVIRONMENT

In this section, we look at three aspects related to environment: the learning environment (social and physical), support for students and resources.

12. Learning environment

There are two main aspects to consider in terms of the learning environment: the social and the physical (or virtual) environment. Teaching, and a lot of learning, takes place in a social environment where teachers and students come together to learn. Even online learning has a social element in terms of interaction between teacher and students through discussion groups and fora. Creating the right environment that is conducive to learning is an important aspect of the teacher's role. Earlier we discussed Maslow's theory that individuals have a natural tendency to self-actualise, and his hierarchy of needs. For learners to reach their potential and self-actualise they need to feel safe, feel like they belong and have self-esteem, so teachers have a role to play in creating the right social environment.

Lave and Wenger (1991) argue that learning is situated within a social context in which individuals experience learning. Students are situated within various contexts for their learning, each of which can be seen as a *community of practice*. A student is part of various communities of practice, such as a school/department, a year group on their degree, a module cohort, etc. A new student will start on the periphery of a school community but as they progress through their degree they become a more central part of that community. Progression onto a postgraduate course would move them further towards the centre occupied by teachers and researchers in the school.

When students do not engage in discussions in a small-group teaching session, consider why this might be. It may be that they haven't done the preparatory work, but it may also be that they feel like an outsider within the group or are shy and lack the confidence to speak out in front of the group. Strategies such as giving students the opportunity to discuss with a partner or sharing answers anonymously can help build their confidence and enhance their self-esteem, which will increase the chances of them contributing more in future. Small-group teaching methods are discussed in Chapter 5.

Related to Maslow's hierarchy of needs, it is important that the physical environment is conducive to learning. Whilst some aspects such as the temperature of the room, lighting and background noise may be outside your control, if you are teaching in a cold room then recognise that you may need to move rooms, provide breaks so students can get up and move or shorten the session. Room layouts are also important in terms of how they encourage or discourage interaction between the teacher and students (Jaques, 2003) especially for small-group teaching methods. For virtual learning environments, the structure, layout and organisation of the website can impact on how students engage with the resources. A site that takes a long time to load or is difficult to navigate will discourage students from using it. Also important is how the site encourages engagement from and interaction between students, and its accessibility for all students, including those with a disability.

Implications for teaching

Teachers need to create a classroom or online environment where students feel part of a group or cohort, can contribute to discussions without fear of being wrong and feel valued. Recognise the group of students you are teaching as part of a community and provide students with opportunities to engage with more experienced members of the community, and serve as a role model. Try and ensure the physical (or virtual) environment is conducive to learning and if it is not, be ready to adapt.

13. Support

As well as creating a conducive social environment for learning, you are also expected to provide academic support and sometimes pastoral support for students. Irrespective of your role, it is important that you know what support services are available to students and are able to signpost them effectively. See Chapter 7 for further guidance on supporting students.

Implications for teaching

Know what your responsibilities are in terms of providing academic and pastoral support for students, and signpost students to relevant support services.

14. Resources

To learn effectively, students need access to the appropriate learning resources to support their learning. Many of these, such as libraries, computer rooms and Wi-Fi, are provided by the institution. There are a whole host of online texts, websites, videos, podcasts and apps that can also be used. Teachers need to consider what resources are available that could enhance student learning, and signpost students to them. It is also important to consider that some students may not have access to their own laptop or the latest smartphone, and access to the internet off campus might be limited. So teachers need to ensure all students are able to engage appropriately in the learning activities set. Teachers are also a resource that students want access to and the main way they get access is through taught sessions and online engagement. Many institutions and schools now require staff to publish office hours each week when students can discuss any academic issues with their teacher. These can be done face to face or online.

Implications for teaching

Ensure that students have access to the resources they need to engage in learning activities and also to you as their tutor.

AND FINALLY

15. Learner autonomy

We started this chapter by considering what we want our students to learn and our graduates to be, and we end it by emphasising one of the main aims of HE, which is to develop independent, autonomous learners who take responsibility for their own learning and can decide what they need to learn and how to learn it and can evaluate how well they have learned. Doing so means that students can go on to use and develop their subject and become independent lifelong learners after they leave university.

Implications for teaching

Encourage students to take responsibility for their own learning and decide what they need to learn and how to learn it, so they can evaluate how well they have learned.

SUMMARY

In this chapter, we have discussed a range of theories on student learning and focused on the practical implications of these for teaching. We have built on a list of things that help students learn developed by Butcher et al. (2020), and conclude with our list of the key things to consider when teaching:

1. Background: find out who your students are, what their background is and what their support needs are.
2. Beliefs: help your students develop their beliefs about knowledge and learning by exposing them to different knowledge ideas, environments and activities.
3. Motivation: recognise that students' motivation to study varies; act as a role model and share your passion and enthusiasm for your subject.
4. Prior knowledge: find out what your students already know and build on those foundations helping them construct their own knowledge.
5. Clear learning outcomes: be clear about what you want your students to learn and ensure learning outcomes, teaching and learning activities and assessments align.
6. Relevance: explain the relevance of what you are teaching (how it fits in the bigger picture) and make connections between current, prior and future learning.
7. Structure of content: identify the key concepts in your subject and provide an organised and sequenced pathway through them.
8. Experience: give your students opportunities to learn by doing (practical activities, case/problem-based learning or work placements) and encourage them to reflect on their learning.
9. Challenge: use tasks, problems and activities to challenge students and scaffold their learning. Provide opportunities for students to work collaboratively.
10. Assessment: design assessments that encourage time on task, focus students on the most important aspects of the course and encourage quality learning.

11. Feedback: ensure regular opportunities for students to receive and discuss specific and timely feedback that will help develop their understanding.
12. Environment: create a learning environment where students feel part of a group, can contribute to discussions without fear of being wrong and feel valued. Try and ensure the physical environment is also conducive to learning.
13. Support: know what your responsibilities are in terms of providing academic and pastoral support for students and signpost students to relevant support services.
14. Resources: ensure that students have access to the resources they need to engage in learning activities and also to you as their tutor.
15. Learner autonomy: encourage students to take responsibility for their own learning and decide what they need to learn and how to learn it, so they can evaluate how well they have learned.

The extent to which these are relevant will depend on your role, and there is no expectation that you adopt all these practices immediately. Many of the aspects discussed will be explored in more detail throughout this book.

FURTHER RESOURCES

Graduate attributes

University of Edinburgh Graduate Attributes Framework – an example of how one university defines what its graduates look like
www.ed.ac.uk/graduate-attributes

Constructivism

The Teachers Toolbox – a website aimed at school teachers but with a helpful explanation of constructivism
www.teacherstoolbox.co.uk/constructivism-a-learning-process-the-teachers-toolbox/

Approaches to learning

Biggs, J.B., and Tang, C. 2011. *Teaching for Quality Learning at University: What the Student Does*. Maidenhead: Society for Research into Higher Education/Open University Press. Chapter 4, Context for Effective Teaching and Learning

Future Learn website with extract from UNSW Sydney's online course, Introduction to Learning and Teaching in Higher Education
www.futurelearn.com/courses/learning-teaching-university/0/steps/26384

Learning theories

Ashwin, P., Boud, D., Coate, K., Hallett, F., Keane, E., Krause, K.-L., Leibowitz, B., MacLaren, I., McArthur, J., McCune, V., and Tooher, M. 2015. *Reflective Teaching in Higher Education*. London: Bloomsbury Academic. Chapter 2, Learning: How do Students Develop their Understanding

Merriam, S.B., Caffarella, R.S.B., and Baumgartner, L.M. 2006. *Learning in Adulthood: A Comprehensive Guide*. San Francisco: John Wiley & Sons. Chapter 11, Traditional Learning Theories

Stewart, M., Understanding Learning: Theories and Critique, in: Hunt, L., and Chalmers, D. (eds). 2012. *University Teaching in Focus: A Learning-Centred Approach*. London: Routledge

Useful summary of the argument against learning styles
www.buildingrti.utexas.org/resource-pages/learning-styles-neuromyth-debunked

Threshold concepts

Land, R., Meyer, J., and Smith, J. 2008. *Threshold Concepts within the Disciplines*. Rotterdam: Sense Publishers

Threshold Concepts: Undergraduate Teaching, Postgraduate Training, Professional Development and School Education: A Short Introduction and a Bibliography from 2003 to 2018
www.ee.ucl.ac.uk/~mflanaga/thresholds.html

12 things that can help learning

Butcher, C., Davies, C., and Highton, M. 2020. *Designing Learning: From Module Outline to Effective Teaching*. Abingdon: Routledge. Chapter 5, Selecting Teaching and Learning Methods

Chapter 4

Curriculum and course design

[UKPSF: A1, K6 & V4]

KEY FINDINGS FROM OUR SURVEY

Forty-six per cent of our respondents are module convenors. The main challenges they faced were:

- Knowing the procedures and how they work in the UK
- How different processes were compared to *home*.

These points were made eloquently by a number of those respondents; for example:

> I found it challenging that I did not have a good understanding of how the course worked as a whole and thus found it difficult to plan.
>
> American lecturer teaching in the UK

> Unorganised teaching structure, no templates, no explanations. It was assumed that any system works like the UK and we were aware of all procedures.
>
> German lecturer teaching in the UK

> The curriculum structure is completely different to what I experienced in Canada and the United States.
>
> Canadian lecturer teaching in the UK

> It would be helpful to receive some materials (e.g., a manual or guidebook 'for dummies') which explain administrative procedures and

CURRICULUM AND COURSE DESIGN

terms, tailored to newcomers from overseas.
American researcher teaching in the UK

One piece of advice that was very clear:

> Make sure to read all policy, the whole quality manual and to ask an experienced colleague before you do anything related to teaching!
> Italian lecturer teaching in the UK and abroad

Whether or not you take a major role in designing aspects of the *curriculum* and/or *courses of study* (we will define these terms in a moment), it is important that you understand how any teaching, support for your students' learning and/or assessing that you are responsible for links to, and ties in with, all other aspects of the students' learning experience. You also need to know how the course(s) that your students are following is/are decided, agreed/approved, managed and changed, and be able to think through the implications that this has for your teaching and managing of student learning. There is an entire book in this *Key Guides* series dedicated to course design (Butcher et al., 2020) and we suggest you check that if you want to find out more. For our purposes in this text the questions that you need to know answers to are:

1. What do we mean by *curriculum* in the UK?
2. How are courses approved in universities?
3. Are there models that help us design teaching and learning experiences for students?
4. How are courses changed?

Whilst we will only be giving outline answers to these questions, we also aim to help you find the fuller answers you need in the institutions where you are working.

WHAT DO WE MEAN BY CURRICULUM IN THE UK?

We wish that there was simple answer to this question but unfortunately there does not seem to be one. As Butcher et al. (2020, p.22) state:

> Today the word is used to describe a range of educational opportunities from the narrow course of study to the all-encompassing totality

CURRICULUM AND COURSE DESIGN

of student experiences that occur in the educational process related to a course at an educational institution.

They go on to describe the *totality of student experiences* in terms of:

- *Taught curriculum*: this covers the degree (or qualification) subject(s)
- *Co-curricular*: learning that complements the chosen degree subject(s)
- *Extra-curricular*: this encompasses learning beyond the course timetable
- *Hidden curriculum*: unspoken or implicit academic, social and cultural values.

We are interested here in the *taught curriculum* so will focus on that, but you need to think about, and take account of, the wider learning opportunities that students encounter and have available to them; we cannot treat our learners as empty vessels when they come to our lecture theatres, tutorial rooms or practical classes.

We are going to focus on the taught curriculum as this takes up the major component of the timetabled course that the students are registered for. Generally, our students are aiming to gain a bachelor's degree (for a full-time student these degrees are typically three years long but may be four if they include a year abroad or in industry, and four/five years in Scotland), master's degree (typically one year long for full-time students) or doctorate (typically three years for full-time students but may include a write-up period), but they can leave with intermediate qualifications, and these are all described within the Frameworks for Higher Education Qualifications of UK Degree-Awarding Bodies that apply in the UK. You may recall from Chapter 1 that there are two frameworks (FHEQ – Framework for Higher Education Qualifications in England, Wales and Northern Ireland; FQHEIS – Framework for Qualifications of Higher Education Institutions in Scotland) and they come under the auspices of the Quality Assurance Agency (QAA), and that in Chapter 1 we distinguished between the *level* of a course and the *year* of a course; if unsure, then please check back.

Progression

More importantly for this chapter, you need to be able to distinguish between levels in order that you can plan for and ensure ***progression*** throughout the taught curriculum. What, for example, is the intellectual difference between a Level 4 course and a Level 5 course? This is a really important question that you need to answer whether you are designing

CURRICULUM AND COURSE DESIGN

a course or planning lectures, other classes and learning materials. The QAA assist here as it has published *level descriptors* (QAA, 2014) and we recommend that you take time to scan that document, particularly sections 3 and 4. You may also find that your own institution gives guidance on this, so it is worth checking.

To exemplify the idea here, we will take a couple of examples from a different, but very helpful, source; the Handbook of the Welsh Higher Education Credit Framework (WHECF, 1996). Table 4.1 shows the increase in expectation across levels 4 to 7 for two intellectual abilities: knowledge and understanding; and synthesis/creativity (you will recall from Chapter 1 that *level* describes the intellectual demand of the course whilst *year* refers to the chronological order that students attend the course). In the boxes, the requirements of the learner are described. As with the QAA level descriptors, just reading one box is not as helpful as reading across the levels, and then you will get an idea of the expected *progression*.

TABLE 4.1 Progression

Level	Knowledge and understanding	Synthesis/creativity
4	Has a given factual and/or conceptual knowledge base with emphasis on the nature of the field of study and appropriate terminology	Can collect/collate and categorise ideas and information in a predictable and standard format
5	Has a detailed knowledge of (a) major discipline(s) and an awareness of a variety of ideas/contexts/frameworks which may be applied to this	Can reformat a range of ideas/information towards a given purpose
6	Has a comprehensive/detailed knowledge of (a) major discipline(s) with areas of specialisation in depth and an awareness of the provisional nature of the state of knowledge	Within minimum guidance can transform abstract data and concepts towards a given purpose and can design novel solutions
7	Has great depth of knowledge in a complex and specialised area and/or across specialised or applied areas. S/he may be working at the current limits of theoretical and/or research understanding	Can autonomously synthesise information/ideas and create responses to problems that expand or redefine existing knowledge and/or to develop new approaches in new situations

(WHECF, 1996, p.11)

It is not possible in a text of this nature and size to consider details of progression in every aspect of the taught curriculum, but hopefully this short example has started you thinking about the idea and will prompt you to ask colleagues and use the resources we refer to in order to help you.

Courses of study

There are several terms used in UK higher education (HE) for courses of study.

- **Course**: a dictionary definition is 'a set of classes or a plan of study on a particular subject, usually leading to an exam or qualification' (dictionary.cambridge.org). Confusingly we also refer to a *degree course*, so you will find this term used in many ways.
- **Module**: a module is a self-contained, sub-unit of a degree that usually runs across one, or at the most two, semester(s). It tends to focus on one subject or aspect of a discipline and usually is assessed independently. Modules usually carry a credit rating (discussed below) and are grouped together to create courses leading to a qualification. Students will often be studying several modules concurrently.
- **Unit**: some universities do not use *module* for the sub-units or parts of a degree but instead use *unit*.
- **Programme**: or, more completely, *programme of study* – these are typically whole degrees (see Chapter 1 for **programme specification**).

Perhaps the most important message from the last paragraph is that you need to check what terminology is used where you are and how the various parts add up to make a course leading to qualification.

HOW ARE COURSES APPROVED IN UNIVERSITIES?

In Chapter 1 we talked about the impact of the QAA and the guidance it provides, and that as a result all institutions will have a quality unit of some type. Typically this quality unit will have a range of responsibilities, and one of them will be to ensure that all taught courses are subjected to detailed peer scrutiny before they are offered to students. There will be a course-approval method that will apply to both full degree courses and to sub-units, be they modules, units or whatever. The procedures will

CURRICULUM AND COURSE DESIGN

require that *subject benchmark statements*, *credit ratings* and *professional body* requirements are taken into account, so we will mention those briefly below, but before that a few more words about approval processes.

Course approval

Invariably there will be *course-approval documents*, be those on paper or online, that on completion will go to a school/departmental committee and then, perhaps, onto a faculty/institutional committee (depending on whether the course is new or a revision and whether it is a full degree or a sub-unit) for scrutiny. Transnational education (TNE) courses will usually have to undergo an additional level of scrutiny in the local country before they are permitted to run.

The sections on the form are likely to mirror the aspects of good course-design models that we introduce later in this chapter, which shows that the process is based on good pedagogic foundations. The approval process may take a couple of iterations if there are questions about the proposal, but after approval the details will be recorded in the institutional catalogue of modules/programmes, etc. We are emphasising the significance of course approval for four important reasons:

1. Once approved, the document becomes the contract between the institution and the (future or current) students on the course and cannot be changed without agreement of the students currently on the course or, for the next cycle of students, without a reapproval process of the change(s) if they are significant (sometimes referred to as *major changes* with the less significant as *minor changes*).
2. The approval process will cover a number of aspects:
    a. For a module/unit this could include learning outcomes, level, credit rating, teaching and assessment methods, how students will receive feedback on assessments (both process and timing), resources (including library- and technology-based) and guidance on directed and independent study hours.
    b. In addition, for programmes of study it will include any benchmark statement(s) that apply, which modules/units must be studied (core) and those that are choices (options), any professional body accreditation and evaluation procedures.

CURRICULUM AND COURSE DESIGN

3. This takes time; a new programme could take a year or more to go through the committees and a new module more than half a year; major changes can take up to a semester, mainly due to the timing and limited frequency of committee meetings.
4. Some colleagues see this as a bureaucratic process but we see it as academic leadership; you are deciding what the graduates of the future in your discipline are learning, and this will profoundly impact on the development of the subject.

The significance of the above to you is:

- Find out what the current approved documents say, and stick to them. In doing so you will also become aware of what the documents require should you be involved in, or lead, the design of or changes to a course.
- Check which are considered *minor changes* in your institution as these can usually be changed without lengthy reapproval by a school/departmental committee (e.g. reading lists and sometimes teaching methods).
- Check which are considered *major changes* in your institution as these can only be changed through reapproval by a school/departmental committee (e.g. assessment methods, learning outcomes).
- Find out what the approval/reapproval process is and the timescale to make changes in order to ensure that you are aware and prepared.
- Remember the importance of this process to the future of the discipline – academic leadership.

If it helps to have an example of this, try webprod3.leeds.ac.uk/catalogue/. This is the link to the *University of Leeds Module and Programme Catalogue* (if the link does not work – as these things sometimes change – just search for the italicised words and you will find it). There you will see for every academic year from way back until now the full list of all undergraduate degree programmes and modules; there is an equivalent list of postgraduate degrees and modules for the same period too. All universities have to make these available, so check the website where you are.

Credits/credit rating

As mentioned above, in the UK it typically takes three years (four in Scotland) to complete a full-time bachelor's degree (BSc or BA), and it is claimed that there is some equivalence across degrees in terms of workload. How do we design our courses so that this is the case? The answer is that we use a tariff – credit – system which:

- Gives credit ratings to units/modules of study
- Sets a total credit requirement for a particular qualification (e.g. 360 for a first degree in England)
- Equates a credit with nominal student workload; one credit = 10 hours of student work.

The most important bit of that was *one credit = 10 hours of student work*, as this is really helpful when you design your course and/or teaching. However, not all HEIs use a credit system, and some use UK credit and others the European credit system (ECTS); it is important, therefore, to check out what is done where you are. Below we give you a simple example to illustrate the value of knowing about credit ratings; if you want to read more see QAA (2008).

A typical 10-credit undergraduate unit or module requires 100 nominal hours of student work, and a 20-credit would be 200 hours. These hours include:

- *Taught/timetabled hours* – lectures, tutorials, practical classes, etc.; these are sometimes called *contact hours*
- *Directed time* – work you set in preparation for classes or after classes, including online (blended)
- *Assessment tasks that do not count* towards the unit/module mark (formative assessment – see Chapter 6 for more)
- *Independent study time* – when the student is free to explore the topic and follow-up their own interests
- *Revision for and completion of assessment(s) that make up the unit/module mark* (summative assessment – see Chapter 6 for more).

These time allowances will be part of the approved course and will be included on the module/programme documentation. You cannot make a major change without reapproval, so check what has been agreed. You need to direct students to use their time most effectively and efficiently and give guidance about your expectations of preparation for, and follow-up on, classes (directed time). This is where the annotated media lists that we discuss in Chapter 5 come into their own. The link between credits and nominal student hours ensures that the workload is both fair

CURRICULUM AND COURSE DESIGN

and appropriate across modules/units/courses of study. We are often surprised to find that teaching staff do not talk about these hours to students, which means, of course, that students do not understand the expectations fully.

We have included more information in the *Further resources* section below, but you should now have an overview of the credit system and the associated study hours.

Subject benchmark statements

We noted in Chapter 1 that the QAA provides subject benchmark statements, and they:

> describe the nature of study and the academic standards expected of graduates in specific subject areas. They show what graduates might reasonably be expected to know, do and understand at the end of their studies.
>
> (QAA, 2020)

All degree programmes in the UK are expected to take account of these statements, so it is worth your becoming familiar with the ones that apply to your discipline (www.qaa.ac.uk/quality-code/subject-benchmark-statements).

Professional, statutory and regulatory bodies (PSRBs)

In order to practice in some professions (e.g. health-related and engineering roles) the degree course has to have been approved/accredited by the appropriate professional body. For example, the starting point for medical doctors in the UK is a degree in medicine that has been accredited by the General Medical Council (GMC). We mention this need for accreditation here only because you may find that there are parts of the degree that you teach that are required for accreditation and cannot, therefore, be changed. These requirements will have been built in when the programme of study was designed and approved at your institution and then a separate accreditation process by the professional body will have taken place. We leave you to check whether this applies to the degree subjects that you teach.

The past couple of pages of this chapter, covering both the external influences of the QAA and professional bodies and the internal course-approval

CURRICULUM AND COURSE DESIGN

process, may have seemed rather dry and abstract. The best way to gain a better understanding of the course-approval process is to look at the approved documents for the courses that you are teaching, talk to an experienced colleague about how the process works in your institution and maybe visit the quality unit and talk to them. As we said above, you will see that the documents mirror the aspects of good course-design models so we will move on to look at those models and consider how they might assist us.

ARE THERE MODELS THAT HELP US DESIGN TEACHING AND LEARNING EXPERIENCES FOR STUDENTS?

The simple answer here is yes; lots of them. However, being pragmatic, the model that will be most influential in your institution is the *course-approval document* that we mentioned above. These documents are based on valid pedagogic principles and models and we will mention two major ones (*constructive alignment* and *Dennis*) here to illustrate the point.

Constructive alignment

In Chapter 3 we introduced the concept of *constructive alignment* (attributed to John Biggs; see Biggs and Tang, 2011) which comprises three stages:

1. Tell the learner what it is you want them to learn:

    The knowledge, skills, approaches and attributes (called the intended learning outcomes)

2. Provide them with the opportunity to achieve these expectations:

    Teaching methods, learning opportunities, resources and formative assessment

3. Test them on their achievement:

    Summative assessment with grades/marks and feedback (current quality) and feed-forward (how to improve).

As you read the above three bullet points, we think you will agree that this is common sense; the learner needs to know what they need to know and be able to do and then you help them achieve this before you test them in a valid way. In *Further resources* we have included some additional reading that expands on this. You will have noticed the mention of (intended) learning outcomes in the first stage; we have talked about these in Chapter 1 and will return to them below. The principle of constructive alignment should underpin all teaching and assessing of students. It applies to a single lecture/class all the way through to the full degree course.

Some colleagues talk about *backwards design*, and to us this is a variation of constructive alignment and what we would call *iterative constructive alignment*, and includes the following six steps:

1. Start with the intended learning outcomes – what the learner should be able to do at the end of the course.
2. Create a list of the essential knowledge, skills and concepts that students need to learn.
3. Design the assessment that students will complete to evidence to what level they have learned and what they can do that decides the final mark (summative assessment).
4. Create a series of teaching sessions and learning activities and opportunities to help the leaner get from where they are to where they need to be.
5. Determine strategies that help learners decide what they have achieved and what is left to do as they work through the course (formative assessment).
6. Check that the plan that results makes sense and is workable.

Both of these approaches are focused on the learning outcomes, teaching and learning approaches and activities and assessment strategies (the essential triad of designing effective courses). However, there is more to think about when planning the full degree and that is where the course-design models, like Dennis, come in.

Dennis: course-design model

We call this the *after*-Dennis model (Figure 4.1), as Norman Dennis proposed the seven headings in workshops for staff on course design in Singapore in the early 1990s. He would probably not recognise the version we use, but the model builds on his original ideas. Butcher et al. (2020) describe several other models, and in *Further resources* the AISHE (All Ireland Society for Higher Education) and Trinity materials are well worth exploring.

CURRICULUM AND COURSE DESIGN

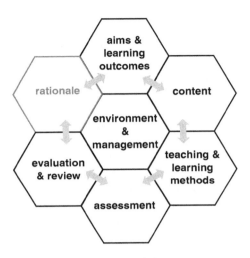

FIGURE 4.1 Dennis, course-design model

We particularly like the Dennis model because: it is *comprehensive* (covers all that you need to think about) whilst being *concise* (there are just seven, reminder headings and one of those is only visited occasionally), *coherent* (it is consistent with other models, incorporates constructive alignment and is clear and easy to follow), *cyclic* (there is a flow from learning outcomes around the model and it reminds us that any change in one aspect will impact elsewhere, so we need to keep that in mind); and *iterative* (the arrows go both ways so that you can go both forwards and backwards in your thinking). We will consider each aspect in turn, but we emphasise that **aims** and learning outcomes should always lead the design process, which is why they are at the apex of the model.

- *Rationale*: you will notice that this aspect is printed in grey rather than black; this is because it is only considered occasionally, whereas all of the other aspects should be reviewed at least annually. By *rationale* we are asking "Why is this degree course (module/unit) being offered?" Once we are clear that it should be, we move on to the other six aspects to determine the details of the programme specification. The rationale for a course could be: there is a market (students who want to attend), it fills a gap in the provision of the school (e.g. a master's course that builds on the strength of the bachelor course), it combines with another strength either in the school or elsewhere to offer

73

CURRICULUM AND COURSE DESIGN

something unique or special (e.g. a joint degree in an emerging discipline), it builds on your cutting-edge research and there is a growing demand for the topic, etc. The important point is that there is a need and a market. We may revisit the rationale after maybe five years to check that there is still a need and market, and this may lead us to confirm it with minor or major changes or cancel the provision.

- *Aims and leaning outcomes*: there are many terms that are used to describe what we expect our students to learn: *teaching objectives, competencies, behavioural objectives, goals*, etc. You will need to check what terminology is used where you are, but we will use *aims* and *learning outcomes* (which are also the QAA-preferred terms). We return to aims and learning outcomes after this overview of the seven components of the Dennis model.
- *Content*: you are the expert here, and so we will not spend much time considering this aspect. However, chapter 4 in Butcher et al. (2020) considers the topic in detail, so apart from reminding you that it is the learning outcomes that drive the selection of content, and not the other way around, we will move on.
- *Teaching and learning methods*: we discuss these in Chapter 5.
- *Assessment*: we discuss this in Chapter 6.
- *Evaluation and review*: we discuss these in Chapter 8.
- *Environment and management*: this is a bit of a catch-all category and includes ways to support students and create effective learning environments (see Chapter 7); how we manage the course, from timetabling classes to giving out information to students; ensuring appropriate and sufficient learning resources (library and IT resources); and providing access to materials and staff (library, virtual learning environment (VLE) and staff office hours). Many of these aspects will be achieved through standard processes and procedures that run in your school/department, and you will need to ask colleagues to find out the information.

Aims and learning outcomes

Aims are broad, general statements of educational intent and should inform students of the overall purpose of a programme, course, module or session. Some of the aims will be discipline-specific whilst others can be seen as general, graduate attributes and employability skills. For example:

CURRICULUM AND COURSE DESIGN

- *The aim of this course is to develop autonomous learners and creative thinkers who have an in-depth understanding of modern educational thinking and have the essential practical and professional skills to become effective teaching practitioners.*
- *The aim of this module is to introduce you to the important components of course design and should enable you to design flexible and coherent modules and programmes fit for a twenty-first-century university degree course.*
- *Today's lecture will introduce you to the value of learning outcomes and give you guidance on how to write them.*

They are often written in provider (lecturer/tutor) rather than receiver (learner) terms. You can see from the examples that they give the broad outline but no detail. After hearing/reading them you know what it is all about (big picture) but not what you actually need to learn and be able to do as a result; that is the role of learning outcomes. Notice the way that the ideas cascade down from the course to the module to the individual session, becoming more specific as one gets to each teaching session; some call this *nesting*.

Learning outcomes, as defined by Butcher et al. (2020, p.48), are

> more focused and indicate what a student is expected to be able to do at various points during and/or at the end of a course of study. Typically, learning outcomes specify the minimum requirement at the point of assessment for the award of credit: threshold requirements. They may refer to subject specific concepts and skills, or more general (transferable/generic) attributes and abilities. Whatever, they should be written in student rather than lecturer terms.

Let us use an example in order to illustrate this:

> *On successful completion of the Postgraduate Certificate in Higher Education, you should be better able to:*

- Critically evaluate different teaching approaches and methods in order to develop your own teaching practice in the light of what is known about learners' needs
- Develop, critically evaluate and implement appropriate assessment and feedback/feed-forward strategies.

CURRICULUM AND COURSE DESIGN

Taking these apart, the first statement applies to all of the learning outcomes and is an essential precursor as it carries many messages:

- *On successful completion*: reminding the learner that this is a partnership and they need to do the learning; we can only support them to achieve, not achieve for them.
- *Postgraduate Certificate in Higher Education*: this reminds us that it is a Level 7 course and so leaning outcomes should match that expectation intellectually.
- *You should be better able to*: setting the expectation, and *should* highlights that there are no guarantees (back to the *on successful completion* point above, as they have to do their part); *better able* reminds us that learners do not come to us as empty vessels — they have experiences and knowledge that they bring to the teaching/learning experiences.

Moving on to the learning outcomes themselves:

- *Critically evaluate*: all learning outcomes have verbs; what the learner should be able *to do*. The learner should be able to *evaluate* (judge, measure), and *critically* typifies high-level outcomes at master's level and signifies comparing and contrasting, justifying and giving a rationale for the evaluation and the judgement.
- *Different teaching approaches and methods*: describes the content that needs to be evaluated.
- *In order to develop your own teaching practice*: again, a verb (*develop*), so the learner knows what they will be doing as a result, but also giving context to the learning; a purpose.
- *In the light of what is known about learners' needs*: more content/context that the learner will need to take into account when critically evaluating.
- *Develop, critically evaluate and implement*: the verbs tell the learner what they should be able to do (develop, evaluate and implement) with the *critically* emphasising at what level.
- *Assessment and feedback/feed-forward strategies*: the content that will be studied and the preceding verbs tell the learner what they need to be able to do with this content. It does not say *know* or *recall*, which is all about knowledge and memorising stuff; it says *develop*, *evaluate* and *implement*, which is about application, analysis and evaluation.

CURRICULUM AND COURSE DESIGN

Learning outcomes should be comprehensive and cover everything that is expected of your learners: the intellectual capabilities (what they know and what they can do with what they know); the expected attitudes, approaches and values (some of which may be disciplinary and others involve professional/general life); and the full range of skills (both subject-specific and more general transferable/graduate attributes). Learning outcomes need to be differentiated; think back to what we were saying about progression and levels earlier in the chapter. Finally, learning outcomes need to be based around verbs – what we want the students to be able *to do*: describe, identify, distinguish, explain, discriminate, construct, summarise, compare, etc.

Newcastle University (2018) provides some useful advice when writing learning outcomes and building on their guidance:

- Use a single, clear action verb for each learning outcome.
- Do not use vague terms such as *know about, be familiar with, understand, be aware of* – these cover such a broad range of meanings that they are useless!
- Write in short sentences to maintain clarity. A learning outcome is much clearer as a number of short sentences rather than one, long, complex sentence.
- Module or course learning outcomes should relate to programme learning outcomes, so check to ensure this is the case (we call this *cascading*).
- There should be a clear link between learning outcomes and assessment, and a learning outcome should not be included if you do not plan to assess it (which may be in another module or unit).
- Ensure the learning outcome can reasonably be accomplished within the timescale of the module/unit or course, and the resources necessary for learning are available.

We would add that it is essential to talk to your learners about the learning outcomes as this can help clarify what is expected and reinforces their value. Learning outcomes are written to guide learners and help them understand what is expected, so they should not be confined to the course handbook. They should be discussed at the start and reviewed at the end of learning and teaching activities, and we should encourage our students to use learning outcomes to guide their effort.

There is a great deal of guidance about writing learning outcomes, and perhaps the most common is based on the Bloom Taxonomy (Bloom, 1956) or the revised version of same (Anderson and Krathwohl, 2001). Butcher et al. (2020, chapter 3 – which includes a couple of useful lists of verbs at different levels) and Butcher in Fry et al. (2015, chapter 6) cover the topic in greater detail. In addition, a simple web search will bring up a plethora of guidance and advice from universities across the world (see *Further resources* below for a few great sites), and you will probably find that either the quality or academic development unit in your institution provides guidance and help. This brings us to the end of the answer to the third question that we posed at the start of this chapter (are there models that help us design teaching and learning experiences for students?), which just leaves the final one.

HOW ARE COURSES CHANGED?

We have addressed this question at different stages of the chapter, and our final advice would be *do not change them*. That is until you have:

- Checked the course (programme and module/unit) documentation that is already approved
- Found out what process for changing courses applies where you are, remembering that it is likely that some changes will be:
    - Minor: can be changed fairly easily and quickly
    - Major: can only be changed via the reapproval process that will include consideration by school or institutional committee(s).

Once you are clear about this information, you can start planning for changes. In Chapter 8 we talk about some of the evidence that might prompt changes that need to be made.

 FURTHER RESOURCES

The UK higher education system – studying in the UK

www.studying-in-uk.org

This is an information and news publishing website about the UK HE sector. Whilst principally aimed at international students, much of the content of the site will be useful background to you also.

study-uk.britishcouncil.org/find/study-options

CURRICULUM AND COURSE DESIGN

This is the British Council site and claims to provide practical information and insight on UK education for international students. The same information will be useful to you, especially the section on study options, but do browse around as there is plenty of other stuff too.

www.collinsdictionary.com

An online dictionary — but this one also includes videos of how to pronounce words; for example, see www.collinsdictionary.com/dictionary/english/module

Contact hours

Explaining contact hours (QAA, 2011)
www.qaa.ac.uk/quality-code/supporting-resources

The QAA provides supporting resources for the Quality Code and there are two publications about contact hours: one for institutions and one for students. Also, the Office for Students (OfS) provides information for students:
www.officeforstudents.org.uk/media/2db81e6b-e4c7-4867-bc5d-ff67539d13e8/guide_to_providing_info_to_students.pdf

Speaking in English

10 English Words You're (Probably) Mispronouncing!
www.youtube.com/watch?v=tw25CM1MXlU

Help to sound like a native speaker in English
www.youtube.com/watch?v=ChZJ1Q3GSuI

Constructive alignment

Aligning teaching for constructive learning
www.heacademy.ac.uk/sites/default/files/resources/id477_aligning_teaching_for_constructing_learning.pdf

A short article outlining the principle.

Biggs, J., and Tang, C. 2011. *Teaching for Quality Learning at University*. 4th ed. Society for Research into Higher Education. Maidenhead: Open University Press/McGraw-Hill Education.

This is the fourth edition with this title (the first three were with Biggs as sole author), and they all include the idea of constructive alignment.

Open educational resources from University College Dublin: Teaching and Learning, Session Plans and Modules, Using Biggs' Model of Constructive Alignment in Curriculum Design
www.ucdoer.ie/index.php/Using_Biggs%27_Model_of_Constructive_Alignment_in_Curriculum_Design/Introduction

This is an interesting page outlining the principle with a thought-provoking example; there are links to some other great resources too …

CURRICULUM AND COURSE DESIGN

Design models

AISHE, 2015. All Ireland Society for Higher Education, Academic Practice Guides 3: Huntley-Moore, S., and Panter, J. 2015. *An Introduction to Module Design.* www.aishe.org/wp-content/uploads/2016/01/3-Module-Design.pdf

The AISHE student-centred, outcomes-based model for module design is interesting as in many ways it mirrors the sections of the Dennis model but starts from the student: student diversity and learning approaches and the context(s) in which they are studying. The resource is well worth downloading, and it is free (see www.aishe.org/aishe-academic-practice-guides/ for more details).

The Trinity Inclusive Curriculum Project has a range of excellent, free online resources to support the development of inclusive modules: www.tcd.ie/CAPSl/TIC/.

For example, on module and programme design:
www.ucd.ie/teaching/resources/moduleandprogrammedesign/

Learning outcomes

Many institutions have local guidance and support materials available to assist colleagues when writing outcomes; we illustrate this with links to five:

1. University College Dublin, Ireland (UCD)
   UCD provides a range of helpful resources.
   www.ucd.ie/teaching/resources/moduleandprogrammedesign/designingprogrammes/aimsandoutcomes/
2. University of Bristol, UK
   The narrative compliments and supports the text above, but also there are links to a number of useful quality-related documents and a video in which an academic talks about mapping the programme learning outcomes to the unit (module) outcomes; the nesting/hierarchy that we discussed earlier.
   www.bristol.ac.uk/academic-quality/approve/approvalguidance/intendedlearningoutcomes/
3. The University of Adelaide, Australia
   Interesting document that ties in the Australian quality agency (TEQSA) Qualifications Framework and graduate attributes (topics discussed in chapters 1 and 2) and yet another approach to writing outcomes: Stem; Active verb; Focus/Object; Context/Condition/Qualifier (optional)
   www.adelaide.edu.au/learning/teaching/resources-for-educators/curriculum-resources/learning-outcomes#outcomes-or-objectives
4. Johns Hopkins University, Baltimore, USA
   Videos rather than words and a summary dos-and-don'ts list. They talk about writing learning objectives (well, you cannot win them all!), including using the use of the Bloom Taxonomy to assist in writing.

They talk about objectives rather than outcomes as the nomenclature can be different in different countries.
https://facultyforward.jhu.edu/learning-roadmap-for-new-online-instructors
5. Vanderbilt University, Nashville, Tennessee, USA
We include this page as it gives links to many other useful resources too.
wp0.vanderbilt.edu/cft/guides-sub-pages/blooms-taxonomy/

Planning a teaching session

www.ucd.ie/teaching/resources/teachingtoolkit/planningateachingsession/

A great resource.

See also Butcher et al. (2020, chapter 5, 100) for an outline teaching plan.

Chapter 5

Teaching for supporting learning

[UKPSF: A2, K2 & V1]

KEY FINDINGS FROM OUR SURVEY

Teaching methods that respondents were involved in:

- Small-group teaching (seminar/tutorial) 81%
- Lecturing 74%
- Supervising undergraduates 54%
- Supervising postgraduate students 51%
- Practical classes 40%.

The main challenges they faced were:

- Engaging students in discussion
- Promoting interaction in all forms of teaching
- Knowing the backgrounds/previous learning of their students.

These points were made fluently by a number of those respondents, who, for example, found the following challenging:

> [T]o engage students in active discussion.
>
> Kazakhstan PhD student teaching in China

> Students don't respond to questions.
>
> Irish lecturer teaching in the UK

Their advice was clear:

> [D]on't teach for exams, try to provide a deeper insight into the subject matter and the relevance of the material in a broad context.
> Irish lecturer teaching in China

> Have passion, and let your passion bloom every time you are in class. Try to always put yourself in the shoes of the student. Be fair to students of all [backgrounds].
> Nigerian lecturer teaching in Malaysia

> Try using more videos and documentaries, visits, talks from experts related to the course to enhance your course.
> Malaysian lecturer teaching in Malaysia

INTRODUCTION

This chapter asks you to think about the teaching methods that you plan to use, why you would select them and what technology might be available to enhance what you do and improve learning gain for students. The title of the chapter is important, as May and Silva-Fletcher (2015, p.333) remind us:

> A humbling truth for all teachers is the fact that what the student does is more important in determining what is learned than what the teacher does.

There are various ways that we can consider the merits and shortcomings of methods, and here we will link back to our discussion in Chapter 4 concerning intended learning outcomes for students: intellectual abilities — what they know and what they can do with what they know; attitudes and approaches; and skills, both motor and generic life and people skills. Table 5.1, derived from Butcher et al. (2020, p.89), lists a range of typical teaching methods used in UK degree courses, and those in bold are discussed in this chapter. In addition, we will consider the value of blended learning (supporting face-to-face, or f2f, teaching with online learning) and online learning, as well as directing you to a number of other resources that might be of interest and help to you.

All learning and teaching is contextual; an important point about the ticks in Table 5.1 is that it is our thinking about the methods in our

TEACHING FOR SUPPORTING LEARNING

TABLE 5.1 Learning outcomes driving selection of teaching methods

	\multicolumn{7}{c}{Focus of the learning}						
	\multicolumn{2}{c}{Intellectual abilities}	\multicolumn{2}{c}{Attitudes and approaches}	\multicolumn{2}{c}{Skills}	Group skills	Oral skills
Method	K C A	A S E	Aware	Habit	Guidance	Expert	Develop	Develop
Lectures	✓			✓				
Tutorials		✓	✓	✓	✓	✓	✓	✓
Seminars	✓	✓	✓	✓				✓
Practical classes		✓	✓	✓	✓	✓	✓	
Role play		✓	✓	✓			✓	✓
Simulations		✓		✓		✓	✓	
Problem-based learning	✓	✓	✓		✓		✓	✓
Projects and dissertations		✓		✓		✓		✓
Online discussion rooms		✓	✓	✓	✓	✓	✓	✓
Learning logs		✓	✓	✓	✓	✓		✓
Case-based learning	✓	✓	✓	✓			✓	✓

K C A – Knowledge, Comprehension & Application (considered as lower-order thinking);
A S E – Analysis, Synthesis & Evaluation (considered as higher-order thinking)

contexts. You need to think about who and where you teach and move the ticks (✓) accordingly if they do not seem to suit, and you may need to add other methods that are commonly used where you are. Having done that, we will now move on to think about making best value of some of the approaches.

LECTURES

Lectures are common in the majority of university courses and are typically timetabled to last one hour, but should only last for 50 minutes, allowing a 10-minute gap between classes for students to arrive from, perhaps, the previous class and leave and get to the next class; they often run from five past the hour until five to the hour. Lectures, depending on the discipline, will often be attended by large numbers of students; as many as 500 students in some departments/schools, but more usually 100–180 in most subjects at undergraduate level.

Why lecture?

The term is derived from the Latin *lectare*, meaning to read aloud; because that is, basically, how the method began. When books – information sources – were scarce, before the printing press, photocopier and tablet, if you wanted to learn then listening to the one who knew, and had the book, was the way forward. We mention this as such an approach – reading aloud from the book – in today's world is totally inappropriate and so we need to think about why one would lecture in 2020 onwards.

We suggest that there are four main reasons for lecturing in higher education (HE) today:

- Coverage of content
- Framework for learners
- Inspiring/motivating
- Role modelling.

Coverage of content: a lecture is an efficient and cost-effective (one-to-many) way to present information. If a shortage of sources of information was the issue hundreds of years ago then the opposite is true today; a Google search for *lecturing* came back with nearly 23,000,000 results in 0.5 seconds. The issues today are: Where to begin? Which are the good sources? Which are the most useful? Part of coverage is about restricting the learners and helping them find the gems in all of that dust. Also, because you know the subject well, you know the most important information that the learner needs to know and the most difficult to come to terms with; so they will need your help to get their head around that *troublesome knowledge* and through those *threshold concepts* (Meyer & Land, 2003 and 2006, and also see Chapter 3). Finally, coverage should include the most recent knowledge and understanding; in universities we talk about research-based learning or research-led teaching and so should include cutting-edge or perhaps yet-unpublished information. But we should not be standing at the lectern reading this content out – more of that later. It is usual to include a reading list as part of the lecture, either at the time as part of the handout (be that printed or, more usually these days, online) or in the module handbook. It may evidence that we know our topic if we give a five-page reading list, but we need to think about the student and how we can support their learning rather than demonstrate our knowledge. Reading lists should be:

- *Differentiated*: you should include materials that helps fill gaps and background for those who are struggling, and stretch materials for those who are succeeding, as well as fleshing out any topic(s) covered in class.
- *Media lists*, not just reading lists: there is so much available in terms of videos, podcasts, articles, books, etc., that you should be including the full range as this also addresses the question of different learning preferences.
- *Annotated*: useful guidance should be given about which to read/watch/listen to depending on their needs; you will know which are easier or harder to read and understand, and sharing this with learners will help them gain an understanding of the authors/producers on the topic.
- *Sufficient*: you want the students to use the list and not be outfaced by it. You can always include further resources in the virtual learning environment (VLE), but at the time of the class you should be focusing on the essentials and need-to-knows.

Framework for learners: there is no way that we can cover everything that the students need to learn in the lecture, and, thinking about those directed study times (see Chapter 4) and the media lists that we provide, the lecture should be giving the students a foundation, framework or scaffold on which to build the rest of their study of the topic. We learn by building connections and remembering key points/hooks, and the lecture should provide the overview on which the detail will hang. We also need to be addressing the concepts and topics that the learners would find most difficult to work on alone; this will give them the basis and confidence for consolidating and extending in the directed-time work.

Inspiring/motivating: we want our students to go out of the lecture buzzing with excitement about the topic, feeling some of the passion that we have for the subject. This should inspire them to dig into that media list. If you are not fired up by the topic then how can you expect them to be?

Role modelling: historians approach problems in a different way to chemists. Linguists think and use language in different ways to engineers. One is not better or worse than another – they are different. Seeing and hearing you talk about your discipline inculcates the learners into the ways of *thinking and practising* within the discipline (Meyer & Land, 2003). This is part of the hidden curriculum, and whilst you may not be thinking about it, you are modelling certain behaviours, values and approaches that typify your discipline.

Lecture how?

If we are clear about *why* we might be lecturing in 2020 onwards then we now need to think about *how* we should lecture. We initiated this thread above by saying *you do not read it out*, and there have been many studies (Stanford, n.d.; Donavan, 2013; Short & Martin, 2011) which tell us the traits and habits of effective lecturers, and building on them these are the characteristics that we think are most important:

- *Has clear learning outcomes* and uses them to structure and support the class. This is not a slide at the start that is not discussed, returned to or valued and is treated like the information about the fire exits. It is a vital part of the class and informs the learners what they are there for and helps them check that they have achieved what is expected of them.
- *Knows their stuff* or at least looks as if they do. They are in command of the content and so have no need for a script and reading it out. They may use the PowerPoint slide to remind themselves, but they can talk around the bullet points, pictures and diagrams and add illustrative case studies and examples.
- *Looks at the students*, maintaining eye contact and developing rapport with their learners. Watching for quizzical looks and responding; seeing the nods and smiles and nodding and smiling back.
- *Encourages engagement with the topic*: asks questions, sets quizzes, uses technology to allow students to ask and answer questions. In this way they keep attention of the learners or refresh attention by the interaction they build into the class.
- *Explains clearly*: has a logical and organised way of explaining difficult ideas and concepts. Knows the pitfalls and helps the students

around them. Recognises that this might be easy for them as the lecturer, but it is new and difficult for their audience; empathises.
- *Uses appropriate technology* to support learning (presentation software – PowerPoint, Keynote, Prezi – that includes more than words), and gains feedback and adds interaction (personal response systems – Turning Point, clickers, Hats Off, etc.).
- *Responsive and flexible*: uses a range of approaches to stimulate interest and explain concepts – talk (modulating voice to add interest), videos, pictures, diagrams, tasks, question and answer sessions, case studies, etc. Also willing to go back if learners show they are not understanding, or add detail if the interest is high.
- *Varies the pace but keeps up the momentum*: a good speed for talking in a lecture is about 120 words per minute, but you should not aim to talk for all 50 minutes; you should pause to add emphasis, speed up and slow down to add interest, but maintain about a 120-word average. If running out of time, the answer is to decide which content to ditch rather than just talk faster, and you should not over-run the time as this makes problems for both your students and colleagues.
- *Tells the story*: draws in the audience with the flow of the ideas and concepts, building on the emotions and enthusiasm for the topic.

Aristotle, some 24 centuries ago, summed this up in three words:

1. *Ethos* (credibility)
2. *Logos* (emotions/appeal)
3. *Pathos* (clarity).

His advice is well worth remembering.

Flipped lectures

When asking why we should lecture in 2020 onwards, some colleagues will say that we should not; we should **flip the class** (Advance HE, 2018b, and Mazur, 2012). If the typical order of a lecture is that the students attend the lecture and then go away and do some follow-up, directed learning (some places suggest that they should be doing two or three hours' work on the basis of each lecture) then the flipped class is the reverse. Technology provides us with the ability to record a *lecture* in a lecture theatre (lecture capture; e.g. Echo360, Coursecast, Mediasite, etc.) or at your own desktop (e.g. Camtasia) and then make this available to students through the institution's VLE (e.g. Moodle, Blackboard). The idea is that the students watch the video prior to coming to class and they can do this in their own time, at their own pace, and review parts of the video to check understanding. Then the class time is spent making use of the ideas and concepts by: answering questions (students asking the lecturer and the lecturer asking the students); case studies that the students work on and discuss with each other, then with the lecturer; answering quizzes as teams or individually; etc. This can still be done in large classes, but now instead of the time in class providing the content, the time is spent processing and thinking about the content. This could, of course, be followed by further directed learning, setting up a learning sandwich of *preparation* (watch the video), *processing* (class activities) and *consolidating* (directed time).

The added value here, of course, is that the students can go away and watch the lecture again if they still have questions, and again when they revise for tests/examinations, so it is win-win. This is the reason that many universities now have **lecture capture** as standard, be that recording:

- A speaker, the presentation slides and audio
- Presentation slides and audio
- Just audio.

This does not have to be part of a flipped approach; it just means that the students have access to the lecture after the event. This, of course, raises the question as to why students should bother to attend the live class if they can watch it later; especially if the lecture is timetabled for nine o'clock in the morning! This means that it is your job to make the live event more valuable than the recording, and this requires you to build in interaction: *active learning*.

Active learning in lectures

We are aware that maintaining students' concentration in lectures is difficult, particularly when asking them to struggle with new and demanding content and concepts. Various research tells us that concentration span in lectures can be as low as seven minutes or as long as 20 minutes; both of which are very short compared to the standard 50-minute class (Bligh, 1998). The answer is, of course, to get the students processing the material by answering short questions, discussing ideas, watching a video, etc. We discuss this in Chapter 3, and Exley (2010) adds lots of details for this idea, as do Exley & Dennick (2008, chapter 8).

Technology in lectures

We have already mentioned some of the options and here will quickly summarise the categories:

- *Audio-visual aids*: presentation software allows us to project printed words, diagrams, pictures, audio and video (but do watch out for any copyright violations). You need to think about particular educational needs when designing your presentations (see Butcher et al., 2020, chapter 7) and do think about going beyond just words on the screen. Do not forget to check out the other kit that may be available to you in the lecture room; the document camera, for instance, enables you to project artefacts and materials and you can even use it like a giant marker board. Search for *58 ways teachers use document cameras* for a host of other ideas.
- *Lecture capture*: recording of lectures, both automatically and on-demand, is now available in many institutions, and these can be made available through VLEs. Similar software exists for recording at your desk, and these recordings allow us to *flip* the class.
- *Interactivity*: the need to engage learners both to maintain attention and involve them in active learning has generated a range of *electronic voting*-type software that can be used on personal devices (phones and tablets) or dedicated hardware. Again, many institutions have decided on a particular approach, and you need to find out about and make use of that technology. You can set questions for the students to answer, and their combined answers can be projected and discussed. You can also invite individual comments (electronic questions) and these too can be displayed either just to you or to the whole class.
- *Laptops and tablets*: many students now carry multiple devices with them, and we can utilise them in class to: search for definitions, explanations and translations of complex concepts; take notes and share them with others; annotate lecture notes and slides; use mobile apps to perform calculations; and experiment with visualisations and simulations, etc. This does, of course, depend on all of the learners having access to appropriate technology; our plans must be inclusive, not exclusive.

We have given a range of other readings and media about lectures in the *Further resources* section, and we will now move on to what typically follows a lecture; smaller-group teaching in seminars and tutorials.

SEMINARS AND TUTORIALS – SMALL-GROUP TEACHING

What are they?

Small-group teaching is common in many UK degree programmes. However, terminology does vary and one department's seminar is another school's tutorial, so check out the terminology in your own university. If pushed we would say that tutorial groups (up to 10 to 15 students) tend to be smaller than seminar groups (15 to 25 students), but the numbers vary considerably and whilst the focus of both is students thinking and talking, in seminars students are often required to come prepared to speak about a particular topic (give a short presentation even), whereas in tutorials they are asked to prepare on a topic and then the talk may be structured, by the tutor, around a series of questions or issues. The most important point is that they are not lectures to smaller groups. For larger year groups of students it is often necessary to run parallel seminar/tutorial sessions with a team of tutors. A challenge for course leaders, in this situation, is to ensure parity and some degree of consistency of experience for the students. In this case, all the tutors may be provided with set readings, pre-prepared discussion questions and/or structured learning tasks, so that each tutor can lead the seminar in a similar way.

Purposes

To help you think about your role in these types of classes, it is worth looking at the rewards and shortcomings of the methods and then think about how you will encourage the former and solve the latter. Building on what Exley (in Butcher and Timm, 2013) reported, the rewards of a good tutorial/seminar can be that they:

- Encourage students to learn actively and to participate in class
- Provide a forum for deeper understanding and more critical engagement with a topic
- Allow the tutor to give feedback and support to individuals
- Require the students to take responsibility for their own preparation and learning
- Facilitate collaboration and group learning
- Develop many forms of communication, and analytical and problem-solving skills
- Allow a greater amount of interaction between teacher and students – it is the place you get to know your students and enable students to learn from each other (peer learning)

- Allow students to explore a topic and, guided by the learning outcomes for the course, take responsibility for their own learning (developing as autonomous learners)
- Allow learning from mistakes with no penalties (a safe environment).

However, the shortcomings of a tutorial/seminar can be that they:

- Require significant investment of resources, especially tutor time
- Depend on the facilitation skills of the tutor and so may be variable in quality
- Need to be organised and well managed to allow discussion, but to also ensure that the specific learning outcomes for the session are met
- Require all students to participate (even shy or quiet people) and be encouraged and supported to do so; this may be a particular issue if some students are non-native English-speakers and less confident about speaking
- May be less effective if all students do not prepare adequately (ensuring students come to class having done their reading or pre-work is a fairly common difficulty, especially in mandatory modules – see below).

An underpinning philosophy in many small-group teaching sessions, as highlighted in Chapter 3, is that the students will learn from, and with, each other (as well as from the tutor). It is likely that your students will come to a particular class with different levels of background knowledge and experience. They will have different interests and views. This mix and variety can be harnessed and used as an additional resource by the tutor to good effect (Falchikov, 2001). However, this learning from peers may not happen spontaneously or naturally. One important role tutors can take is to underline, re-state or reinforce a useful contribution made by a student – this will encourage collaborative learning and help the students see each other as people they can learn from. One example of this is the great international mix that is typical in universities; drawing on students' views and backgrounds can add a transnational dimension to the class and so enrich the outcomes.

Facilitating

You will have realised from the list of rewards and shortcomings above that the skills of the small-group tutor are very different from those of the lecturer, and are often labelled *facilitation skills*. These include (Brown, 1991) the skills of:

- *Questioning*: to seek information, explore feelings and attitudes and encourage thinking
- *Listening*: going beyond what is heard to find out its significance
- *Responding*: including building on answers, asking related questions praise/encouragement, summarising, probing and confronting
- *Explaining*: a temptation is to explain too much too early; explaining should be used rather sparingly and usually in response to a student's answer or comments.

To which Exley et al. (2019) would add:

- *Presence*: alert, aware and receptive to the group and the environment/emotions
- *Humbleness*: students are part of the learning resource and equality rules; all contributions are valued
- *Pleasure in subject*: this goes without saying, but is harder to maintain if you have to repeat the session multiple times; just remember that it is the first time the students have explored the ideas and concepts and you should enjoy their freshness rather than make them suffer your staleness
- *Curiosity for the subject*: academics thrive on research, asking questions and being curious about their discipline, so bring this joy into your teaching – take the opportunity to learn from and with your students
- *Authenticity*: students soon spot a performance rather than the real thing; you need to be you.

Preparation for class

Many tutors spend the first part of the first meeting with a new small group agreeing **ground rules**, which include ways in which the group will behave towards one another and agreeing to prepare. The important point is that these rules apply to both teacher and taught, so preparation by you is essential too:

- Have clear aims and learning outcomes
- Design appropriate learning tasks which will require students to engage actively, possibly by

TEACHING FOR SUPPORTING LEARNING

- ☐ Providing a structured worksheet
- ☐ Devising a set of seminar questions or problem to solve
- ☐ Deciding a topic for a debate
- ☐ Collecting questions for a quiz.

Getting all the students to prepare properly is a common concern for tutors. Approaches that people use include:

- Setting pre-seminar reading which is very specific and has accompanying questions or tasks associated with it (rather than just providing extended reading lists)
- Beginning seminars with a quick factual quiz that checks basic understanding of the preparatory work
- Requiring students to submit brief summaries or questions before the class, perhaps via a VLE such as Blackboard or as a group-shared email
- Giving specific roles or tasks to individual students (or groups of students) before the seminar. For example, "Could group A be prepared to present the viewpoint of the East and group B lead on the Western view?", or "Could student A take notes here and could student B scribe feedback on the markerboard?"

There are many ways in which we can help our students to gain the best value from small groups and there are some very useful study sites that you can direct them to; we have included some of these in the *Further resources* section.

Online small-group teaching

Finally, some of you may be tutoring online to both distant and local students as the use of VLEs has become commonplace. This has led to a rise in the opportunity to conduct learning online and the need for teachers to develop their skills as e-tutors or e-moderators. Some of the tutorials will be **synchronous** (when students and tutor are online at the same time and conduct virtual conversations in real time) and others **asynchronous** (when students and tutor are not necessarily logged on at the same time; e.g. a student may pose a question and the tutor or other students reply at a later date). A difficulty with online tutoring is that, unless synchronous and supported with video, we only have the written (typed) words to go on, and miss out on the clues and cues that we are used to when talking f2f; so think carefully about your use of language and always build in opportunities for learners to clarify and question at all stages. Gilly Salmon (2002, 2003) has written extensively on the design and implementation of e-learning and has developed a five-stage model to prompt us to think about how to engage our learners most effectively even at a distance (for a quick introduction, see www.gillysalmon.com/five-stage-model.html):

1. Access and motivation
2. Online socialisation
3. Information exchange
4. Knowledge construction
5. Development.

Colleagues talk a lot about *icebreakers* in small-group settings and refreshers in lectures when teaching f2f; here are some ways to break the online ice:

- Choose an emoticon that sums up how you feel today
- Post a picture of where you are working or where you would like to be working
- Say what you are missing about being f2f
- Or more positive, say what advantage there is to be online rather than being f2f.

CASE-BASED LEARNING AND PROBLEM-BASED LEARNING

Whilst case-based learning (CBL) and problem-based learning (PBL) are forms of small-group teaching and learning, they have particular features that it is worth spending a few moments thinking about as versions of both are used in a range of subjects.

The aims of CBL and PBL are:

- Motivating learners
- Knowledge creation, organisation and assimilation
- Development of problem-solving skills and reasoning processes
- Development of team-working skills and behaviours
- Development of self-directed/*lifelong learning* skills.

Although they share common goals, each instructional design possesses unique characteristics:

- PBL – the problem drives the learning
- CBL – requires students to recall previously covered material to solve cases.

PBL is more common in the health sciences (medicine, veterinary science, etc.), whilst CBL is used across the disciplines (engineering, health-based subjects, business and economics). PBL works best as a whole-curriculum approach; students need to learn how to be problem-based learners as they need to work together to find out the basics of a subject in order to solve the problem. The tutors in this format act as facilitators to help support rather than directing the groups, whereas using a case to illustrate, extend and apply learning that has happened in other teaching formats (lectures, seminars and practical classes) does not require the same sort of research and interdependence of the students. The tutor in this case facilitates the groups but also can act as a source of information/ expert witness and be more directive and supportive of the process. If you are expecting to be involved in these formats then see *Further resources* for a couple of brief, explanatory articles and a student-view video and a newsletter that will keep you updated.

PRACTICAL CLASSES

Most undergraduate programmes taught in the sciences, engineering and medical areas include practical and/or laboratory work. Studios or workshops take place in some other subjects; e.g. architecture, design and dance. Practical teaching is likely to account for the majority of a student's contact time with teaching staff in these subjects.

The overall aims of the practical components could, depending on subject, include:

- Subject-related cognitive (scientific method in the sciences and clinical reasoning in medicine, for example)
- Subject-related practical – including professional attitudes
- Key skills – which would be transferrable to other aspects of study and employment.

Other aims might include:

- Skills

- ☐ Analysis of data/information
- ☐ Recording data or procedures
- ☐ Designing experiments/protocols
- ☐ Ethics of experimental design
- ☐ Report writing and intelligent presentation of results (depending on audience)

- Familiarity with kit, procedures and approaches
- Social abilities – working within a group towards a common goal and sharing results/outcomes
- Illustrative knowledge – of theory
- Ability to peer critique.

If you wish to consider this more, Boud et al. (1986) provided a comprehensive list that was developed by Baillie et al. (2017), and a paper by Davies (2008) includes many valuable ideas, particularly in engineering and sciences.

In the first year, students are usually asked to follow procedures and protocols to familiarise themselves with basic methods and equipment. In later years they will be expected to design and plan their own experiments and investigations, which could ultimately conclude with the students undertaking a major piece of individual project work (see *Supervising projects and dissertations* below), and so it is essential that we develop students' ability to, and confidence in, designing protocols and experiments as they progress across levels of the course. The underpinning educational theory for practical work is that of experiential learning or *learning by doing* (see Chapter 3). This means that they also need to be able to cope with, and learn from, failure.

Important questions we need to ask ourselves are "How do we learn a skill?" and the corollary "How do I teach a skill?" if an essential outcome of practical and laboratory works is key skills development. George and Doto (2001) suggested a simple five-step method; they, as medics, were focused on clinical skills but we have generalised their approach:

1. Overview, including *why*: to be motivated to learn a skill, the learner must understand why the skill is needed and how it is used.
2. Tutor demonstrates as a competent person would do: demonstrating the skill exactly as it should be done without talking through the procedure. This silent demonstration gives students a mental picture of what the skill looks like when it is being done correctly.
3. Tutor demonstrates slowly and talking through: repeating the procedure but taking time to describe in detail each step in the process

TEACHING FOR SUPPORTING LEARNING

will help students see how each step fits into the optimal sequence. Allow time for students to ask questions or seek clarification.
4. Students talk through whilst tutor does: asking students to describe step by step how to do the skill will ensure that they understand and remember each step in the correct sequence.
5. Students do with tutor feeding back: students are ready to do their first attempt at the skill with the tutor carefully observing and providing feedback or coaching as needed.

Depending on the discipline, practical sessions may run over part or a whole day and be supervised by academic staff, laboratory technicians and postgraduate demonstrators. One of the challenges for academic staff is therefore to coordinate this extended team. If you are part of the team, note how the leader briefs and supervises the group, in order to develop your skills; this will prepare you for when you take over a team. See *Further resources* for a detailed and valuable resource concerning tutoring and demonstrating in practical classes from the University of Edinburgh.

SUPERVISING PROJECTS AND DISSERTATIONS

In the majority of UK undergraduate degrees, students will undertake a substantial project or dissertation in their final year. This is considered to be an essential part of the course, not only in the importance it receives in the allocation of marks, but as a highly valuable learning experience very much appreciated by employers (graduates are frequently asked about their final-year project in detail at job interviews). The project or dissertation, often regarded as the ultimate **synoptic assessment**, may comprise 40 or even 60 credits in the final year. Similarly, master's degrees by research can be entirely by project/dissertation, whilst taught master's will include a large project/dissertation taking up as much as one-third or one half of the course.

Projects/dissertations are individual and sustained pieces of work which require critical and in-depth study by students. They are usually supervised by a member of academic staff who is often working in an allied or similar research field. The time allocated to supervision varies enormously, and you need to talk to colleagues to find out norms in your context.

Topics for project/dissertation may come from staff (you list areas/titles that you can supervise, and students select from the list) or may be negotiated (students go to staff with an idea and agree a title). In either case you need to be clear about your role in the process and ensure that the task is realistic and achievable in the time available. The project/dissertation may be either *empirical* (new data and evidence are generated, which may involve practical or simulation work and hence ethical considerations may need to be explored and permissions gained) or *non-empirical* (sometimes described as library-based, which does not generate new data; rather it synthesises, criticises and builds on existing knowledge and understanding). In laboratory-based sciences, students are likely to work in their supervisor's laboratory, and resources may include space as well as equipment and funding for chemicals or other consumables. In arts and social sciences, students may need to use texts and primary sources that have controlled access that staff can facilitate.

Whilst the work is going to be done by the student and your role is to monitor and support, it is worth thinking about all of the aspects of the project/dissertation to ensure appropriate supervision:

- Identifying a clear question to be answered
- Sourcing the relevant information:
    - Knowing what has already been done (if anything)
    - Checking the validity and reliability of sources
    - Evaluating the evidence from all perspectives
    - Collecting/creating more evidence/information
- Synthesising the known and the new and coming to a decision/conclusion
- Presenting the outcomes of the work:
    - Critically
    - Articulately
    - According to conventions of the discipline.

Building on Exley (in Butcher and Timm, 2013), we think that it is good practice to establish and agree supervisory arrangements in a supervisory contract; a checklist for drawing up such a contract should include:

- How often and for how long will you meet
- Who organises the meetings
- How meetings will be recorded and by whom
- The schedule of meetings, perhaps related to the stages of the work:
    - Title/purpose of the project/dissertation
    - Timescale and work schedule
    - Sources of resources/information
    - Research method, if appropriate, and ethical review
    - Writing-up

- How you can be contacted between supervisory meetings
- Your role = supervisor not doing the project/dissertation
- How you will provide feedback and on what.

Ensuring professionalism – exchanging agendas, keeping brief minutes, recording agreed actions and deadlines – helps set the tone for the supervision and can also be important if difficulties arise later and the student either fails to meet deadlines or fails the project assessment. If there is an appeal against your supervisory practice, this sort of this documentation will be essential. In *Further resources* we have listed some excellent texts that add to this topic.

BLENDED/ONLINE LEARNING

In various places in this chapter we have discussed the use of technology to support teaching and learning. The difficulty is, of course, that with the fast-moving pace of technological advancement, both in everyday life and education, this book may be out of date before it is published. However, even though the technologies and tools may change, the principle of the mix – the blend – of f2f and online teaching and learning (e-learning) will remain. Butcher and Timm (2013) provided a comprehensive list of the advantages of e-learning, and we build on that list to ask you to think about the way you will blend the two approaches.

- *Flexibility of time, pace and place of study*: students can study at their own pace in their own time and preferred place of work, and revisit content as often as they wish and need.
- *Media-rich learning materials*: you can provide students with links to useful online resources (texts, sound recordings, animations, simulations and videos) and use multi-media content developed by yourself and elsewhere. Remember the copyright rules.
- *Extending contact*: either synchronous or asynchronous, you can supplement traditional, f2f contact between students and between students and yourself (discussion rooms, blogs, wikis and interactive classrooms allow students to meet with their peers and tutors virtually, ask questions, work collaboratively, share reflection and keep a record of discussion).
- *Support preparation*: providing pre-lecture reading, videos or interactive content; using discussion rooms and formative assessment; collecting questions to be answered in lectures.

TEACHING FOR SUPPORTING LEARNING

- *Flip the class*: by asking students to engage with content prior to f2f contact, more class time can be made available for discussion, answering questions, group activities, *active learning*, etc.
- *Reinforce learning*: by providing opportunities for practice, self-assessment and revisiting content.
- *Encourage enquiry*: by students' use of online tools for research, reflection and collaboration.
- *Provide formative assessment*: online assessments; e.g. quizzes and tests that give immediate answers and feedback.
- *Provide feedback*: online marking tools, making feedback available electronically, or using audio or video feedback.
- *Improve administration*: making announcements, providing timetables and time-release content.
- *Encouraging good academic practice*: tools can check for copying, plagiarism and cheating.
- *Meeting expectations*: students are used to technology being an integral part of their learning in schools and their daily lives and enter HE expecting the same.

Moving online

Some of you will be aware that all levels of education were impacted across the globe in early 2020 by COVID-19, and this resulted in all f2f classes being cancelled and schools, colleges and campuses closing and courses moving online. As a result, a lot of good ideas were shared about how to make online teaching and learning work as well as possible; we have collected a few of the best and include them in *Further resources*.

To conclude, we started by asking you to think how you would select the teaching methods you use on the basis of the intended learning outcomes for your students; learning driving the teaching. We have surveyed a number of common teaching methods and looked at their particular strengths and causes for concern. We now leave you with further resources that extend each of those topics and remind you of the question built into the chapter title: *How will you teach in order to support learning?*

 FURTHER RESOURCES

We include additional readings and media that you can consult if you wish. Please notice that we have annotated some of the resources, as we suggested above.

101

Flipped learning

harvardmagazine.com/2012/03/twilight-of-the-lecture

Harvard Magazine news article in which Eric Mazur talks about interactive teaching. Then search for him: there are several videos where he talks about the flipped classroom.

flippedlearning.org

A series of resources – US secondary-based, but comprehensive.
www.youtube.com/watch?v=BFbqo_zHKpI&feature=youtu.be

A video – aimed at secondary in the US – but useful to start you thinking.
www.advance-he.ac.uk/knowledge-hub/flipped-learning-0

Advance HE – a flipped learning resource.
www.youtube.com/watch?v=BCIxikOq73Q

Flipped Classroom Model: Why, How, and Overview. What we like about this one: it uses animation software (e.g. VideoScribe, Animaker) to tell the story.
www.techsmith.com/blog/lecture-capture/

The complete guide to lecture capture in 2020 – a blog resource that is growing.
uwaterloo.ca/centre-for-teaching-excellence/teaching-resources/teaching-tips/planning-courses-and-assignments/course-design/course-design-planning-flipped-class

Ideas on why and how to flip.

Lectures

Bligh, D. 1998. *What's the Use of Lectures?* 5th ed. Bristol, UK & Portland, USA : Intellect Books.

This is a collection of the research on lecturing; a meta-study. The original text (1972) is the source of many of the tried and tested ideas used by effective lecturers – the latest edition brings these up to date and adds more.

Exley, K., and Dennick, R. 2009. *Giving a Lecture: From Presenting to Teaching.* 2nd ed. Abingdon: RoutledgeFalmer.

One of a series of key texts designed for those who are about to start teaching – a great book that has a lot of practical advice and ways to improve practice, with supporting rationale.

Fry, H., Ketteridge, S., and Marshall, S. 2015. *A Handbook for Teaching & Learning in Higher Education.* 4th ed. Abingdon: Kogan Page.

Chapter 7 by Ruth Ayres talks about the *why* and *how* of lecturing – worth a read for consolidation, examples and useful questions to ask yourself. There is a later, fifth edition that has other ideas and views on the topic.

Swanwick, T. (ed.) 2014. *Understanding Medical Education: Evidence, Theory & Practice.* Chichester UK & New Jersey USA: Wiley Blackwell.

Chapter 10 Lectures and Large Groups by Andrew Long and Bridget Lock discusses a range of issues that are particularly pertinent to medical and veterinary scenarios.

And some online resources:

- www.ucd.ie/teaching/resources/teachingtoolkit/deliveringalecture/
- www.ucd.ie/teaching/resources/teachingtoolkit/largegroupteachingstrategies/
  Two from a range of useful resources from University College Dublin.
- www.bumc.bu.edu/facdev-medicine/files/2010/06/Lecturing.pdf
  A great summary and guide for refreshing lectures.
- www.schreyerinstitute.psu.edu/tools/
  Some great resources from the USA – use *lectures* or *lecturing* as your first search term.
- serc.carleton.edu/serc/site_guides/largeclass.html
  More resources for teaching large classes.
- www.honolulu.hawaii.edu/facdev/teaching-techniques/
  This site is well worth a visit as it covers far more than lecturing.
- staff.brighton.ac.uk/clt/Pages/CurrDev/Teaching.aspx
  Centre for Learning and Teaching, University of Brighton: lecturing.

Online

First, online resources and then ideas about moving classes from f2f to online.

Film, video and radio resources

Many of us use films, TV and radio programmes in our courses. Box of Broadcasts (BoB) currently has over 2.2 million copyright-cleared broadcast programmes available to stream, and over 120 universities and colleges are subscribed. Check whether your institution is a subscriber and then go search: learningonscreen.ac.uk/ondemand.

Television and Radio Index for Learning and Teaching (TRILT) bufvc.ac.uk/tvandradio/trilt/

Simulations and online laboratories

Biochemistry
www.ucl.ac.uk/~ucbcdab/simulations.htm

Earth Sciences
The virtual microscope: www.virtualmicroscope.org

Science Education Resource Center at Carleton College: serc.carleton.edu

TEACHING FOR SUPPORTING LEARNING

Physics and Astronomy
ComPADRE: www.compadre.org

Science and Mathematics
Phet interactive simulations: phet.colorado.edu

Researcher resources online

These require that your institution has a subscription – it is worth checking.

Angel Productions (for doctoral students): www.angelproductions.co.uk/universities.htm

Vitae: www.vitae.ac.uk/doing-research

Moving teaching online

At the start of the COVID-19 pandemic in 2020, a number of institutions shared a range of resources to help academics move their f2f courses online. They were still available when this text was written, and hopefully many still are.

How to Be a Better Online Teacher: Advice Guide

www.chronicle.com/interactives/advice-online-teaching

Flower Darby offers some good advice.

Engaging Online Students

Thanks to Panos Vlachopoulos, Macquarie University, Sydney, Australia.
lt.arts.mq.edu.au/teaching-support/online-delivery-resources/engaging-online-students/

Home-made videos to help academics

Thanks to Virna Rossi, educational developer based in London, UK.
vimeo.com/showcase/6967044

They cover:

- Basics
- IT
- Adapting teaching and assessment
- Supporting students.

One book that was ahead of this rush to online offers some good advice:
Stein, D.S., and Wanstreet, C.E. 2017.. *Jump-Start Your Online Classroom: Mastering Five Challenges in Five Days.* Sterling, Virginia: Stylus Publishing.

Keypath Education

keypathedu.com/elevate

Currently Keypath is offering 10 videos to help *faculty* (it is US-based) get online, and they are aimed at all levels of education. We have included them as the quality and production of the materials themselves give great ideas, never mind the messages the videos convey. We may not have such great production facilities available to us on campus but it is worth thinking about the impact that can be gained by going beyond the talking head and a few PowerPoints.

Pearson (publishers)

Advice to students
www.pearson.com/uk/learners/higher-education-students/he-student-blog.html

We are not sure this resource will remain open, but Pearson is always worth checking out. If the link breaks, search for its HE student blog.

Massive open online course: Learning to Teach Online

Produced by the University of New South Wales, Sydney.

> The Learning to Teach Online (LTTO) MOOC will help you develop a working understanding of successful online teaching strategies that you can apply in your own practice. The course is based upon the multi award winning open educational resource developed by Dr Simon McIntyre and Karin Watson.

It is offered, free, through Coursera: www.coursera.org/learn/teach-online.

The Difference Between Emergency Remote Teaching and Online Learning

An article by Hodges, C., Moore, S., Lockee, B., Trust, T., and Bond, A.: er.educause.edu/articles/2020/3/the-difference-between-emergency-remote-teaching-and-online-learning

This includes online learning design options (moderating variables), ideas adapted from Means, B., Bakia, M., and Murphy, R. 2014. *Learning Online: What Research Tells Us about Whether, When and How.* New York: Routledge. You will see *Educause* in that web address. It aims to advance HE through the use of IT (www.educause.edu).

Problem-based learning and case-based learning

Wood, D.F. 2003. ABC of Learning and Teaching in Medicine: Problem Based Learning. *BMJ.* 326, 328–330.
A concise but comprehensive article.
Azer, S.A. 2005. Challenges Facing PBL Tutors: 12 Tips for Successful Group Facilitation. *Medical Teacher.* 27(8), 676–681.
The title gives away the content; a useful read if you are new to the approach.
A student vlog at Maastricht University www.youtube.com/watch?v=HTF3QOjscbc

A collective student view from Maastricht University
www.youtube.com/watch?v=7n_Rzwc-ZNU
Maastricht University, internationally renowned for PBL, has a number of videos on YouTube that give different and positive perspectives.

The *Case Centre Connect* is a free newsletter that will keep you up to date with what's happening in the case community and provide you with details of new and popular teaching materials being used worldwide. Launched in January 2012 it is now sent to over 52,000 subscribers worldwide.
www.thecasecentre.org/educators/casemethod/resources/connect

Practical classes

Tutoring and Demonstrating: Handbook. University of Edinburgh.
www.ed.ac.uk/institute-academic-development/learning-teaching/staff/tutors-demonstrators/resources/handbook

Edited by Forster, F., Hounsell, D., and Thompson, S. The original version was published in 1995.

Seminars and tutorials

Exley, K., Dennick, R., and Fisher, A. 2019. *Small Group Teaching.* Abingdon: Routledge.
This is the second edition of this great book (the first edition is worth checking out too), full of ideas which are supported by research and theory.
Fry, H., Ketteridge, S., and Marshall, S. 2015. *A Handbook for Teaching and Learning in Higher Education: Enhancing Academic Practice.* London: Kogan Page.
Chapter 10 Effective Online Learning, Chapter 11 Challenging Students: Enabling Inclusive Learning, and Chapter 12 Encouraging Independent Learning are all valuable. This text also includes, in Part 3, examples from the disciplines.
Habeshaw, S., Habeshaw, T., and Gibbs, G. 1992. *53 Interesting Things to Do in Your Seminars and Tutorials.* Bristol: Technical and Educational Services.

Yes, a very old book but one that is full of ideas of ways to get learners active and thinking.

Hartley, P., and Dawson, M. 2010. *Success in Groupwork*. London: Red Globe Press.
This is an essential resource for all students who are expected to produce a group project as part of their course, regardless of their level or discipline.

Jaques, D., and Salmon, G. 2007. *Learning in Groups: A Handbook for Face-to-Face and Online Environments*. 3rd ed. London: Kogan Page.
This edition covers supporting small groups of learners both f2f and online.

Lublin, J., and Sutherland, K. 2009. *Conducting Tutorials*. New South Wales: HERDSA. https://www.herdsa.org.au/publications/guides takes you to the

This is one of many Higher Education Research and Development Society of Australasia guides, all of which are short and to the point and full of useful information. This one is targeted at small groups in the social sciences but is still a valuable resource.

Race, P. 2000. *500 Tips on Group Learning*. London: Kogan Page.
Lots of ideas in one book.

And some online resources:

- www.ucd.ie/teaching/resources/teachingtoolkit/smallgroupteachingstrategies/
  One of a range of useful resources from University College Dublin.
- www.advance-he.ac.uk/knowledge-hub/working-students-teams-or-groups
- www.advance-he.ac.uk/knowledge-hub/small-group-teaching-toolkit-learning
  Advance HE – good resources but the website often changes, so just go searching.
- https://teachingcommons.stanford.edu/online-teaching-guides
  This page lists the Stanford online guides – the class activities provide a range of good ideas.
- www.bumc.bu.edu/facdev-medicine/files/2010/06/small-group-teachng.pdf
  Small-group methods; written for medics but covers it all and applies to most disciplines.
- www.ucd.ie/t4cms/ucdtlt0021.pdf
  Describes promoting participation methods in detail.
- www2.le.ac.uk/offices/ld/resources/study/contributing-seminars-tutorials
  University of Leicester, Student Learning Development. Contributing to seminars and tutorials. Guidance for students on how to make the best from small-group teaching; many institutions have pages like this.
- staff.brighton.ac.uk/clt/Pages/CurrDev/Teaching.aspx
  Centre for Learning and Teaching, University of Brighton: seminars.

Supervising projects and dissertations

Fry, H., Ketteridge, S., and Marshall, S. (eds). 2004. *A Handbook for Teaching and Learning in Higher Education*. 2nd ed. Abingdon: Routledge.
See Chapter 8 on supervising projects and dissertations.
Fry, H., Ketteridge, S., and Marshall, S. (eds). 2015. *A Handbook for Teaching and Learning in Higher Education*. 4th ed. Abingdon: Routledge.
See Chapter 13 on supervising research degrees.
Wisker, G., Exley, K., Antoniou, M., and Ridley, P. 2008. *Working One-to-one with Students: Supervising, Coaching, Mentoring and Personal Tutoring*. Key Guides for Effective Teaching in HE. Abingdon: Routledge.

Technology-enhanced learning

www.ucd.ie/teaching/resources/technologyenhancedlearning/

Chapter 6

Assessing and giving feedback

[UKPSF: A3, K2, K6, V1, V2]

KEY FINDINGS FROM OUR SURVEY

Eighty-one per cent of respondents are involved in assessing students. The main challenges they faced were:

- Understanding the different system for allocating marks
- Knowing what was expected of them in terms of assessment
- A lack of advice on how to prepare and deal with assessments.

These issues are illustrated by some respondents:

> My main challenge was getting familiar with the British education system from teaching, assessment, rules and regulations.
>
> Iranian lecturer teaching in the UK

> Marking is difficult because of the different level of requirement between countries, I was used to a different education system.
>
> Spanish PhD student teaching in the UK

Others advised:

> Become familiar with the grading schemes and expectations, as they are quite different from in Canada.
>
> Canadian lecturer teaching in the UK

> Plan ahead for your teaching, and more importantly the marking deadlines.
> Egyptian lecturer teaching in the UK

INTRODUCTION

Assessing can mean different things in different contexts. In the UK higher education (UK HE) context **assessment** means making a judgement about some aspect of a student's work and is usually followed by giving the student some *feedback*; i.e. information about their work with a view to helping them improve. The purpose of the assessment may be to guide and encourage learning (e.g. giving feedback on a draft) or may involve allocating a mark or grade that will then be used to make an overall judgement about a student's ability. One of the challenges in writing this chapter and for new international teachers is that there are a whole range of terms used, sometimes interchangeably, to describe aspects of assessing and giving feedback. To help you, some of the key terms are explained in Table 6.1 and others can be found in Chapter 9.

Assessing and giving feedback to students is a key part of the teaching role and one that many who are new to teaching find very stressful because it involves making judgements on students' work. For those new to teaching in the UK, the approach to assessment may be very different to the approach taken in their own country, making it even more challenging. Ultimately, assessment is how we judge students and determines what the overall outcome of their degree is, which can influence their future. Hence it is a high-risk activity for students, assessors and the university. However, assessment is not just about making final judgements on student learning. As discussed in Chapter 3, assessment has a significant influence on students' learning in terms of what, how and how much they study (Gibbs and Simpson, 2005). In recent years, there has been a move away from seeing assessment as just the end-point assessment of learning and instead seeing assessment as an integral part of the learning process (Brown and Race, 2012). This view is endorsed by the Quality Assurance Agency (QAA), which states that:

> Assessment is a fundamental aspect of the student learning experience. Engagement in assessment activities and interaction with staff and peers enables learning, both as part of the task and through review of their performance. It is a vehicle for obtaining feedback. Ultimately, it determines whether each student has achieved their course's learning outcomes and allows the awarding body to ensure that appropriate standards are being applied rigorously.
>
> (QAA, 2018, p.2)

Assess and give feedback to learners is the third of the five areas of activity in the UK Professional Standards Framework (UKPSF; see Chapter 1) and is described as being about how you:

- Assess and give feedback to learners, to foster and encourage their learning
- Assess learners' progress and make judgements about their learning during and on completion of their study with you.

(UKPSF, 2011)

There are also four questions in the annual National Student Survey (NSS) of final-year undergraduate students which relate to assessment and ask students to grade the following aspects:

8. The criteria used in marking have been clear in advance
9. Marking and assessment has been fair
10. Feedback on my work has been timely
11. I have received helpful comments on my work.

(NSS, 2019)

Perhaps not surprisingly, these questions have received lower student satisfaction ratings compared to other aspects of teaching and learning. In 2019 the student satisfaction score for assessment and feedback was 73%, which is well below the overall satisfaction score of 84%. This has been a similar trend since the survey began, so clearly students do not feel that the way in which they are assessed and receive feedback is as good as other aspects of teaching and learning. Hence assessing and giving feedback is an important aspect of teaching and learning for students, staff and institutions. Unfortunately, some of our survey respondents received no support for this aspect of their role:

> total lack of support and induction for non-British lecturers to understand the system (marks, scaling).
> Iranian lecturer teaching in the UK

> We also had no training or guidance with learning how to mark essays and reports. I feel a bit sorry for the students whose work I marked in the first semester or two.
> Australian teaching associate teaching in the UK commenting on when he taught as a PhD student

ASSESSING AND GIVING FEEDBACK

TABLE 6.1 Assessment terminology

Assessment	Process of making a judgement on some aspect of a student's work and therefore their learning.
Assessment criteria	Identify the aspects of the *assessment task* that will be taken into account when the assessor marks the work.
Assessment task	A general term that covers any assessment a student is asked to do; e.g. coursework, exam, test, as defined below:
	Coursework – assessment task done by a student in their own time (not under controlled conditions) during their course. Also referred to as assignments.
	Examination – assessment task completed under controlled conditions; i.e. with a set time and venue.
	Test – assessment task completed in-class or online in semi-controlled conditions and often with a shorter duration than exams.
Feedback	The process of giving a student some information about their work with a view to helping them improve.
Grading	Grouping students' work into bands of achievement and awarding a symbol (e.g. A, B, C) to represent a larger-scale judgement such as overall performance on a course.
Marking	Awarding a number (usually) or symbol to represent the student's achievement, normally in an individual piece of work rather than the overall course. Also referred to as scoring.*
Moderation	A checking process to make sure *assessment criteria* have been applied appropriately and *marking* is fair and consistent.

* In reality the lines between marking and *grading* are often merged because sometimes a piece of work is awarded a numerical mark and at other times a grade.
(Adapted from Bloxham and Boyd, 2007; Sadler, 2005)

Your role in assessing students

The extent to which you are involved in assessing students will vary depending on your teaching role. You may be involved in:

1. Giving students feedback on their learning/progress
2. Marking and giving feedback on a coursework assignment that you may or may not have designed
3. Marking an exam question that you may or may not have written

4. Designing a coursework assignment for a module you are teaching
5. Writing an exam question for a topic/module you are teaching
6. Second marking or moderating an exam or coursework.

You may be the sole assessor or be working as part of a team of markers, so, if you do not already know, find out who else is marking and how that will be managed. Often postgraduate students and researchers are only involved in 1, 2 and 3 in the list above and have not been involved in designing the assessment, but this is also often the case for new academics who have inherited a module (and its assessment) from a colleague. Academic staff may be in roles such as programme director or module leader, where they have the power to alter assessments. However, this normally means going through curriculum-changes approval at school and sometimes university level so can take some time; e.g. up to a year (see Chapter 4). Irrespective of your role, all those involved in assessing need to have at least a basic understanding of assessment and feedback in HE, so we shall start by examining the key concepts. We shall then look briefly at the common assessment methods used before focusing in more detail on marking and feedback. We shall conclude the chapter with a section on how you prepare your students for assessments and one on writing exam questions as this is something many new staff are often asked to do soon after appointment. For advice on designing all other assessments, refer to another book in this series, *Designing Learning: From Module Outline to Effective Teaching*, by Butcher et al. (2020).

KEY CONCEPTS IN ASSESSMENT

In this section, we shall examine some of the key concepts that underpin the whole assessment and feedback process in UK HE. Even if you are not involved in designing assessments, it is important that you understand these concepts.

Norm- v criterion-referenced assessments

Norm-referenced assessment is where the judgement of a student's work is made in comparison to other students in the group; i.e. ranked. Student marks are distributed across the range (normal distribution curve), so it may be that only 5% of students get the top grade; e.g. an A. With *criterion-referenced assessment*, the judgement is made against a set of pre-determined criteria such as learning outcomes, percentage grades,

ASSESSING AND GIVING FEEDBACK

qualitative criteria, etc. So if there are certain criteria for an A grade and 50% of your students achieve those criteria then they would all get an A. In UK HE the module or topic **learning outcomes** are stated (see Chapter 4) and the assessment assesses how well the student has achieved those outcomes, so this is criterion-referenced assessment. In reality, however, markers often compare students' work and make judgements about whose work is better than others' in meeting the criteria, hence there is an element of norm-referencing going on.

Summative, formative and diagnostic assessments

Summative assessments are used to measure a student's learning at the end of a block of learning or a module. A mark or grade is awarded which forms part of a judgement about the student's work and influences whether they can progress or what classification of award they gain. So essentially it is an *assessment of learning* and usually takes place at the end of the learning. Hence *summative assessment* and *assessment of learning* have been used interchangeably. So, for example, if your students do a coursework essay part-way through your module and an exam at the end, and the marks from both of these are used to calculate their module mark, then these are both summative assessments.

Formative assessments, on the other hand, are aimed at giving students feedback about their learning. Even if a mark or grade is generated, it does not contribute to the summative assessment of the module. Instead it is used to help students understand where they are at in terms of their learning (Irons, 2007), and has also been described as *assessment for learning*. This type of assessment generally takes place during the learning, and indeed many have argued that this approach ensures that assessment is an integral part of the teaching and learning process (Pokorny, 2016). So in the example above, before the students have to submit their essay (summative assessment), you might give them a shorter essay to do earlier on and give them feedback on their essay-writing style. This is a formative assessment which provides the learner with formative feedback that they can use to help them with their summative assessment.

Diagnostic assessments are used prior to or at the start of a course or period of learning to ascertain what students already know about the topic. This can be used by the teacher to help decide how to structure the teaching and learning activities.

Before the recent growth in UK HE, lecturers often gave students feedback on their work between classes; for example, on laboratory reports, worked examples and essays. However, the massive growth in student numbers led to a reduction in these formative feedback opportunities and an over-reliance on summative assessment. This resulted in students having fewer opportunities to learn from formative assessments and becoming more focused on the outcome of learning; i.e. the summative assessment mark. There has been much work done in recent years to try achieve a better balance between formative assessments which drive student learning (assessment for learning) and summative assessments which measure learning (assessment of learning). For further information see another book in this series, *Enhancing Learning through Formative Assessment and Feedback* (Irons, 2007).

Validity, reliability and transparency

The *validity* of an assessment relates to whether it assesses what it is meant to assess. Simply stated, if you want to assess students' oral presentation skills then the assessment should be an oral presentation rather than a written report. Likewise, a multiple-choice exam may be a valid method to assess knowledge and comprehension but may not be a valid assessment of the student's ability to synthesise information. However, it is often more complex than these examples. How do you assess critical analysis in an exam with unseen questions and no resources to draw upon? Also, it is easier to assess knowledge and understanding than the higher-order thinking skills such as analysis, synthesis and evaluation, but it is important to do so. If you are involved in designing assessments then this will be a key thing to consider.

The *reliability* of an assessment task relates to whether the same judgement would be reached at different times (by the same marker), by different markers and even by different methods; e.g. if a learning outcome was assessed via a coursework essay rather than an exam question. Various approaches such as learning outcomes, assessment criteria and marking rubrics (see *Marking* below) are often used to try and ensure greater consistency between markers. However, much of what is assessed in HE does have some element of objectivity and relies on the tacit knowledge of the assessor, so it is inevitable that there will be some variability between markers.

The *transparency* of an assessment relates to making it clear to students what it is they are expected to do and by what standards they will be assessed. This does not mean giving them the answers but does aim to ensure that it is not guesswork for students.

ASSESSMENT METHODS

In this section, we shall briefly consider what the typical methods of assessment are in UK HE as these may be different from your own experience of assessment. The predominant forms of assessment in many UK HE institutions are still essays, reports, unseen written exams and multiple-choice tests (Brown and Race, 2012). However, in recent years there has been a diversification of assessment methods for various reasons; i.e. assessing a range of skills and abilities, ensuring students can play to their strengths, etc. All of these have advantages and disadvantages for students and assessors. Table 6.2 lists some of the main methods and is based on a more extensive list in Brown and Race (2012, pp.79–84).

In reading the following sections, it may be helpful for you to think about how the advice given relates to the types of assessments you are likely to be involved in.

MARKING AND FEEDBACK

Before you engage in marking and giving feedback to students it is important that you consider:

- What is the end point for students on the course? At the end of their degree, what will they come out with in terms of a mark, grade and classification?
- How is student work assessed at your institution? Is it marked based on percentages (%), grades (A, B, C, etc.) or classification?
- What contribution does an assessment make to the overall module mark or degree mark?
- What are you expected to do in terms of marking and feedback to students?
- What is your institution's assessment policy on anonymous marking, marking turn-around times, late penalties, resubmissions, academic misconduct, etc.?

In this section we shall discuss the general answers to these questions. However, most institutions and academic schools have an assessment policy which will provide the specific answers for your context, so take time to familiarise yourself with the policy.

The different types of qualifications offered in UK HE were identified in Chapter 1. Whilst various assessments will be carried out over the duration of the degree programme these are usually collated into one overall

ASSESSING AND GIVING FEEDBACK

TABLE 6.2 Assessment methods – advantages and disadvantages

Assessment method	Advantages	Disadvantages
Essays	Requires students to construct an argument and tests writing skills	Rarely used outside education, lot of marking time, easy to plagiarise
Unseen written exams, time-limited	Fair – tests students' own work, avoids plagiarism, yields a quantitative mark	Measures what comes out of student pens/heads, lot of marking and short turn-around time
Reports	More authentic than essays for employment	Often based on data collected in groups but report written and marked individually
Multiple-choice questions	Excellent for quick testing of factual knowledge, feedback can be given instantly	Difficult to design questions that test higher-order thinking or for summative assessment
Practical exams	Tests students on practical skills sometimes in authentic contexts, can be quite quick	Designing good practical assessments can be quite difficult
Presentations	Good for assessing presentation skills alongside subject knowledge	Time-consuming to assess, difficult to get balance between content and presentation skills
Projects	Allows in-depth studies and develops research skills, greater autonomy for students	Varied focus of project can influence reliability of assessment
Viva voce – individual oral tests or interviews	Allows assessor to probe understanding, widely used for high-stakes assessments (e.g. PhD), authentic	Nerves may affect some students, evidence of achievement is short-lived, difficult to achieve fairness between students

(Based on Brown and Race, 2012)

degree classification or grade. One of the challenges for new teachers is understanding what these overall end-points mean.

> My main challenge was figuring out the different grading scales and what grades such as 2:1 or 2:2 actually meant.
>
> Canadian PhD student teaching in the UK

ASSESSING AND GIVING FEEDBACK

The degree classifications for undergraduate honours degrees in the UK are normally based on the percentage marks shown in Table 6.3, although this may vary from one institution to another. In the event that a student does not reach the requirements for a third-class honours degree they may be awarded a pass degree (without honours) or an ordinary degree, but this can only be done if there is a separate programme specification for the ordinary degree. Practice in this will vary so check your own institution's regulations.

For master's-level degrees the pass mark is 50% for students, and at the end of the course students may be awarded one of the classifications of pass listed in Table 6.3, but that does depend on the institution so you will need to check what the rules are for your institution.

It is also important to know how the marks from the modules you teach contribute to the overall degree classification. So, for example, first-year undergraduate marks often do not count towards the final degree classification and therefore students only need to pass to progress, whereas the average mark at the end of the second year may contribute a certain percentage of the student's overall degree mark. Some final-year modules are larger than other modules, sometimes carrying two to three times the number of credits, and hence will have a significant bearing on the overall degree classification.

TABLE 6.3 Typical marking scales

Honours degree class	Percentage mark	Also described as	Shown as	Grade
First-class	70–100%	First	1st	A
Second-class upper	60–69%	Two, one	2:1 or 2(i)	B
Second-class lower	50–59%	Two, two	2:2 or 2(ii)	C
Third-class	40–49%	Third	3rd	D
Fail	<40%			Fail
Master's degree class				
Distinction	70–100%			
Merit	60–69%			
Pass	50–59%			
Fail	<50%			

Marking

Marking and *grading* were defined in the terminology guide (see Table 6.1). In general, in the UK *marking* is used to refer to the process of awarding a numerical mark or grade to student work, so this is how we will use the term here. The marks or grades are collated across the course to work out the overall degree classification.

Before marking a piece of work you need to know:

- What were the students asked to do (and what learning outcomes are being assessed)?
- What are the assessment criteria?
- How are you expected to mark/grade the work?
- What are the penalties for late submission of work?
- When do marks and feedback need to be returned?
- What about students with a disability?
- What if I suspect academic misconduct?

What were students asked to do?

According to the QAA, assessment procedures should be transparent and clear to students (QAA, 2018). Information about what the students were asked to do is usually contained within an assessment briefing or module handbook or guide. This should outline the task that students have been set and any specific requirements. Ideally, it should state which of the module learning outcomes are being assessed, but this is not always explicitly stated. It is important to make sure your students know what they are being asked to do and have the opportunity to ask questions to clarify their understanding. This could be done during a class or online via discussion boards.

What are the assessment criteria?

The assessment criteria identify what aspects of the assessment task will be taken into account when the assessor marks the work. Examples of assessment criteria for an essay might include knowledge of topic, clarity of argument, structure, creativity, use of examples and reference to literature. So, for example, if the structure of a report is one of the criteria then poor structure will result in a lower mark for that aspect. The relative weighting of different criteria may also be specified, so structure might be worth 10% of the marks. The criteria should also make clear whether it is the product (essay, report, etc.) that is being assessed, or the process (group working, communication skills, problem solving, etc.) or a mixture of both. The assessment criteria should be included in the assessment briefing so that students know what aspects of their work will be assessed. However, simply sharing the criteria with students does not mean that there is a shared understanding and will not necessarily result in enhanced learning and more reliable marking (Pokorny, 2016). This is why preparing students for assessment is an important aspect of teaching, which we shall discuss later in this chapter.

How you are expected to mark/grade the work?

Approaches to this vary in different institutions and from course to course. Many use some form of marking scheme or rubric that combines the assessment criteria for that work with the relevant standard – e.g. level descriptors – and outlines what is needed to meet that particular grade. See Table 6.4 for an example of grade descriptors for an undergraduate essay exam. Marking rubrics are more detailed as they include the assessment criteria and a definition of each criteria at each level (class or grade) and usually have some scoring system to indicate the relative importance of that criterion (See *Further resources* for more information). Whatever approach is taken, details should be shared with students in advance, and time spent ensuring students understand the scheme.

As the earlier quotes in this chapter have illustrated, it can be quite challenging for new international staff to adapt to the UK approach to marking and degree classification. One of the issues with the approach is that markers of essay-type questions tend to focus on the middle range of marks – i.e. 35–75% – rather than using the full range of 0–100%, and this can come as a surprise to international staff used to a different approach (Butcher and Timm, 2013). The use of assessment criteria and marking rubrics helps encourage markers to mark across the full range, but tradition sometimes limits this.

Many institutions have an *anonymous marking* policy, which means that students' names do not appear on submitted work, so you will not know who produced the work you are marking. The rationale for such policies is to ensure that there is no bias in the marking process. According to Pitt and Winstone (2018) many of these policies were introduced following a 2008 campaign by the National Union of Students, "Mark my words, not my name", after a survey showed that 44% of students believed that there was some bias in how work was

TABLE 6.4 Example of grade descriptors

Mark (%)	Class or grade	Examination – essay question
90–100	1st class	Outstanding answer. Unequivocal evidence of originality. Explicit evidence of extensive reading, abstracted and integrated to inform answer.
80–89	1st class	Exceptional answer in terms of structure and content. Critical appraisal of literature and data. Some original material. Well-defined arguments presented. Thorough consideration of all dominant and associated issues.
70–79	1st class	Perceptive answer incorporating all dominant issues. Logical development of arguments which are all supported by relevant literature. Evidence of extensive reading. Synthesis of relevant aspects of literature. Lucid presentation.
60–69	2:1	Accurate structured and coherent answer. Most of the dominant issues discussed. Clear development of arguments. Literature used to support some arguments. Limited critical analysis.
50–59	2:2	Answer correct, but not comprehensive. Superficial treatment of subject. Some arguments presented, but not developed. Breadth and depth lacking. Some small factual errors. Very limited reading. Competent writing.
40–49	3rd class	Poorly structured, ill-defined answer. Descriptive approach. Conceptual and factual errors. Insufficient detail. Little evidence of reading.
30–39	Fail	Essay question not adhered to. Answer unstructured. Significant proportion of answer irrelevant. Lack of coherency. Limited understanding of topic.
20–29	Fail	Incomplete answer. Much material irrelevant or incorrect. Limited attempt to answer question. Tendency for repetition and listing of facts. No obvious structure to answer.
10–19	Fail	Relevant material very limited. Structure vague. Partial attempt to answer questions, but information listed and undeveloped.
0–9	Fail	Question not answered. Fragments of relevant pieces of information incidentally included.

(From Butcher et al., 2020, pp.126–127)

assessed. However, others argue that anonymous marking has a detrimental effect on the learning value of feedback and the relationship between staff and students (Pitt and Winston, 2018). Suffice to say that if there is an anonymous marking policy at your university then you need to adhere to that.

What are the penalties for late submission of work?

There is usually a fixed date and time by which coursework assessments need to be submitted, and often there is some sort of penalty for late submission of work; e.g. a percentage deduction from the mark awarded. It is usual that the work is marked in the normal manner first and then the penalty deducted afterwards so students know what mark it was worthy of, but check out the policy at your own institution.

When do marks and feedback need to be returned?

Most institutions now have regulations regarding the turn-around time for marking which are based on the time between the submission deadline or exam date and when the results and feedback are released to students. This is to ensure that feedback comments are provided in sufficient time to allow students to improve their performance in subsequent assessment tasks (QAA, 2018).

What about students with a disability?

As mentioned in Chapter 1, the Equality Act (2010) sets out certain requirements for HE institutions (HEIs) to ensure that they take an inclusive approach to education. Institutions are expected to make reasonable adjustments for staff and students with a disability. In terms of the marking process, most institutions have a system whereby students can indicate to the assessor that they have a specific learning difficulty such as dyslexia. Often students have some form of sticker (real or virtual) that they attach to their submitted work which tells the assessor that the student has dyslexia so the assessor must take this into consideration when marking and giving feedback on the work. There is a growing trend towards designing inclusive assessments so that there is less need to make individual adjustments for students with a disability. For further information about inclusion in teaching and assessment, see Chapter 15 of Ashwin et al. (2015).

What if I suspect academic misconduct?

As with any education system, UK HE has certain expectations of students and indeed staff in terms of the work they produce and the originality of it. *Academic misconduct* has been defined as

> any inappropriate activity or behaviour where a student has attempted to gain, or help another student to gain, an unpermitted academic advantage in a summative assessment.
>
> (University of Nottingham, 2020)

The main types of academic misconduct are:

- Plagiarism (presenting someone else's work as your own)
- False authorship (submitting work that has been written by someone else)
- Collusion (working too closely with someone else then presenting the work as your own)
- Misconduct in examinations (copying from another student or using unpermitted material)
- Making up data, or fabrication (claiming to have qualifications or have carried out work that you have not)
- Failure to obtain ethical approval.

Many institutions now require student work to be submitted via plagiarism-detection software (e.g. Turnitin) to check for any matching with academic sources and other student work.

When marking student work, you will be expected to identify and deal with any instances of academic misconduct but must follow your university policy. The approach taken in the UK can be very different from those in other countries where copying the work of others might be seen as flattery and appropriate. As a new teacher at a UK HE institution, your employer should make sure that you are aware of the regulations around academic practice, not just for your own work but also as a teacher. If you have not been given this information, ask!

Giving feedback

As part of your role in teaching and assessing students you will be expected to give students feedback on their learning, and this is one of the most important yet controversial aspects of the assessment process in UK HE. Students regularly report dissatisfaction with the feedback that they get and yet most teachers argue that they give detailed feedback to students. Part of this issue is undoubtedly around different perceptions of what feedback is. Students may perceive feedback as purely the written comments on their summative assessment, whereas teachers often give feedback during teaching sessions; e.g. group feedback in a lecture after an assignment, or formative feedback in seminars, tutorials or practical classes throughout the module when teachers circulate and discuss student work and ideas with them.

As we mentioned in Chapter 3, feedback is a critical part of the learning process and students need to know how they are doing and what they need to do to improve. So as teachers we need to ensure that we build regular opportunities for feedback into our teaching that will help students develop their understanding. Nicol and Macfarlane-Dick (2006) outlined seven principles for good feedback practice:

1. Helps clarify what good performance is (goals, criteria, expected standards)
2. Facilitates the development of self-assessment (reflection) in learning
3. Delivers high-quality information to students about their learning
4. Encourages teacher and peer dialogue around learning
5. Encourages positive motivational beliefs and self-esteem
6. Provides opportunities to close the gap between current and desired performance
7. Provides information to teachers that can be used to help shape the teaching.

(p.205)

In another book in this series, Haines (2004) talks about a simple strategy called the *feedback sandwich*. This is when you start the feedback by saying something positive about the work and then highlight any issues and areas of improvement before concluding with a positive comment. The idea here is that if you start with positive comments, students are more likely to continue reading and consider your other comments. If you start with negative feedback, students may stop reading.

Feedback methods

There are a variety of feedback methods that are typically used for summative assessments. Written comments, either on a script or on a feedback form, is one of the most common methods. This can be a very time-consuming process and there is evidence that students do not always read their feedback, so it can be frustrating for staff. Feedback pro formas are often used to reduce the time spent giving feedback and can include free text boxes for each criterion, some sort of scale to indicate the standard achieved for each of the criteria, summary statements about what was done well and what could be improved, or a combination of these. Many schools or programmes have a standard feedback form for all assessments, which you have to use, so it is important to find out if there is such a form.

With the advent of online submission of coursework in many institutions, some lecturers have developed comment banks that include a range of statements that the marker can use to annotate the script with a number or symbol relating to the statement. Whilst these can save a lot of time, they can de-personalise the feedback in a manner that students do not like. There are various software packages – e.g. GradeMark (see *Further resources*) – that enable markers to insert a mixture of standard and personalised comments on the online script and can speed up the marking process.

If you are involved in marking exam papers, it is worth checking what the expectations are in terms of feedback. Traditionally, students never got to see their exam scripts (except in cases of appeal) and therefore teachers did not need to write any feedback on them. However, approaches to this have changed and students may now be given the opportunity to see their exam scripts, often in a tutorial with the teacher. In this case feedback comments on the exam script are important. Even if you do not have to write feedback comments, you may be expected to add comments to justify the marks you have given, so it is worth finding out what is required.

Feedback on summative assessments can also be given orally to an individual or group. Many students would welcome one-to-one oral feedback and most staff would love to have the time to do this, but with large student numbers this is often not feasible. Whilst it is possible in some contexts and with small class numbers, there are alternatives such as recording oral feedback online that can help make the feedback more personal. As mentioned in Chapter 3, there is growing interest in the notion of feedback being a dialogue between teacher and learner rather than being something that teachers give learners. Sometimes lecturers provide an opportunity for students to come and see them to discuss their feedback. This is often during *office hours*; i.e. set hours each week where the teacher is in their office and students can drop in to see them.

Many students complain that by the time they get their feedback, they have already moved on to the next module and therefore the comments are of little help. So when commenting on students' work it is important to not just focus on the strengths and weaknesses in that particular assessment (feedback) but also to make comments about how the student can improve their work in future (feed-forward); e.g. *In future essays it is important that you draw on the literature more extensively to support your arguments.* This type of feed-forward comment is essentially giving formative feedback on a summative assessment, so not just giving feedback to justify the mark but also to enhance learning.

Making formative assessment a central part of your teaching and students' learning enhances the opportunities for students to gain formative feedback on their learning. Encouraging dialogue with students and between students during smaller group sessions such as seminars, tutorials and practical sessions is a good way to do this.

Ultimately, we want students to be less dependent on feedback from teachers and move to a position where they can judge their own work (Light and Cox, 2001) so engaging in self-assessment and peer assessment is a valuable way to achieve this. For further advice and guidance please refer to Irons (2007).

Moderation, exam boards and external examiners

As part of the quality-assurance process, once you have submitted your marks for an assessment it is usual for there to be some form of internal **moderation** process before marks are released to students. *Internal* means that it is done by someone within the institution as opposed to an external person from outside the institution. The manner in which moderation is carried out will vary but can include:

- Sample marking by an internal second marker
- Additional marking of any borderline marks, firsts (or distinctions for postgraduate students) and fails
- Additional marking where there is a discrepancy between different elements for a particular student or between different markers.

Depending on your role, you may have some of your marking internally moderated or be asked to do internal moderation for another module. There should be a clear procedure for this, which is normally included in the assessment policy for your school/department or quality-assurance regulations for the university.

Exam boards are usually held once or twice per academic year and may be for one specific degree course (especially if it is a large course) or a group of courses. The exam board is a meeting where results for students are presented and decisions made regarding degree classifications and progress of students from one level to the next. At other institutions, there may be module boards and programme boards held separately, so find out how it works at your institution.

Each degree course also has an *external examiner* who normally reviews a sample of the marking for the course and attends the exam board. The external examiner is an academic from another institution whose role is to provide impartial advice on the academic standards and quality of assessment. They also identify examples of good practice and areas for improvement.

PREPARING LEARNERS FOR ASSESSMENT

Earlier we discussed the importance of ensuring students understand what they are being asked to do.

Providing students with clear details about the assessment (assignment brief), assessment criteria and marking scheme is essential to ensure students have the basic information they need about the assessment.

There is often an assumption that markers and students share an understanding of the assessment process.

> However there is no evidence that simply having assessment criteria and sharing these with students has any impact on the effectiveness of their learning nor on the reliability of marking.
> (Pokorny, 2016, p.77)

Hence there has been a lot of work done in recent years exploring various strategies to help engage students to ensure there is a shared understanding of the assessment task and what will be assessed and how. See Price et al. (2012) in *Further resources* for more guidance on *assessment literacy*.

Beyond this, it is important for you as the teacher to know the context of this particular assessment and how it relates to the previous learning and assessment of the students. If, for instance, one of the assessments on your module is a presentation, you need to find out whether this is the first time they have been assessed via a presentation or if they have done some before. If it is the first time then preparation

ASSESSING AND GIVING FEEDBACK

activities might be as simple as devoting some time to what makes a good presentation or looking at examples of some good and not-so-good presentations (if you can find them). You may even arrange a practice presentation (formative assessment), which may be peer-assessed. If the students have done presentations before, you need to discuss with them how this presentation may be similar or different from ones they have done before. Likewise, *mock* exams can help prepare students for summative examinations. So preparing students for assessment is important both in terms of ensuring they understand how they are being assessed and in terms of supporting them to be successful.

WRITING EXAM QUESTIONS

In the final section of this chapter, we will briefly look at writing exam questions. Although we have not set out to cover the design of assessments in this text, if your module is assessed via an exam then you are likely to be asked to write some or all the questions for it. The format of the exam will probably have already been set so you will need to follow that format. Writing exam questions is a challenging task for all new staff, especially as sometimes you are asked to produce the questions before you have actually taught the entire module.

> There are many things about HE in UK that I did not know about . . . [including] procedures for preparing, approving, marking and moderating exams.
>
> American researcher teaching in the UK

> I did not have any of these inductions before starting my teaching here, and it was very stressful . . . having to get the exam ready in week 2.
>
> Chinese lecturer teaching UK HE in China

In most HEIs, there will be a standard process for production and checking of exam questions. This usually involves the module leader or tutors drafting the questions, some form of internal peer review and often also review by the external examiner. Exam questions are a high-stakes aspect of your work because a mistake in an exam can lead to real issues with student progression and awards, so you are advised to:

ASSESSING AND GIVING FEEDBACK

- Find out what the procedure is for writing and checking exam questions in your school or department
- Check what format your module exam should follow
- Review past papers to see the types of questions previously set
- Draft some questions and share them with a more experienced colleague
- Then follow your school/department procedure.

SUMMARY

Assessment is a critical part of UK HE, not just because it is how degree classifications are determined but also because it has a significant influence on what and how students learn. Ensuring students have regular opportunities to receive and discuss specific and timely feedback that will help develop their understanding is an important part of the teacher's role.

 FURTHER RESOURCES

Assessment and feedback (general)

Advance HE's Transforming Assessment in Higher Education website www.advance-he.ac.uk/guidance/teaching-and-learning/transforming-assessment#projects

Assessment in HE Network, focused on developing research-informed practice in assessment and feedback in HE www.ahenetwork.org/home-3/

Biggs, J.B., and Tang, C. 2011. *Teaching for Quality Learning at University: What the Student Does*. Maidenhead: Society for Research into Higher Education/Open University Press. Chapters 10–12.

Bloxham, S., and Boyd, P. 2007. *Developing Effective Assessment in Higher Education: A Practical Guide*. Maidenhead: Maidenhead: Open University Press.

Butcher, C., Davies, C., and Highton, M. 2020. *Designing Learning: From Module Outline to Effective Teaching*. Abingdon: Routledge. Chapter 6, Designing Assessment and Feedback Opportunities.

JISC. 2020. The Future of Assessment: Five Principles, Five Targets for 2025 www.jisc.ac.uk/reports/the-future-of-assessment

NUS Assessment and Feedback Benchmarking Tool www.nusconnect.org.uk/resources/assessment-and-feedback-benchmarking-tool

QAA UK Quality Code Advice and Guidance – www.Assessmentwww.qaa.ac.uk/quality-code/advice-and-guidance/assessment

Queens University in Kingston, Canada, has a good website on assessment www.queensu.ca/teachingandlearning/modules/assessments/08_s1_05_reflection.html

University College Dublin (UCD) has a useful resource on assessment and feedback www.ucd.ie/teaching/resources/assessmentfeedback/

Assessment literacy

Price, M., Rust, C., O'Donovan, B., Hindley, K., and Bryant, R. 2012. *Assessment Literacy: The Foundation for Improving Student Learning.* Oxford: Oxford Centre for Staff and Learning Development.

Assessment methods

Brown, S., and Race, P. 2012. Using Effective Assessment to Promote Learning. In: Hunt, L., and Chalmers, D. (eds). *University Teaching in Focus: A Learning-Centred Approach.* Abingdon: Routledge.

Formative assessment and Feedback

HEA Feedback Toolkit www.heacademy.ac.uk/sites/default/files/resources/feedback_toolkit_whole1.pdf

Irons, A. 2007. *Enhancing Learning through Formative Assessment and Feedback.* Abingdon: Routledge.

A blog about digital tools and apps teachers can use to support formative assessment in the classroom: www.nwea.org/blog/2019/75-digital-tools-apps-teachers-use-to-support-classroom-formative-assessment/

Inclusive assessment

Ashwin, P., Boud, D., Coate, K., Hallett, F., Keane, E., Krause, K.L., Leibowitz, B., MacLaren, I., McArthur, J., McCune, V., and Tooher, M. 2015. *Reflective Teaching in Higher Education.* London: Bloomsbury Academic. Chapter 15, Inclusion.

Disability Rights UK on Adjustments for Disabled Students www.disabilityrightsuk.org/adjustments-disabled-students

Marking

10 Steps for Creating Marking Rubrics www.plymouth.ac.uk/uploads/production/document/path/11/11370/Guidance_for_Creating_Marking_Rubrics.pdf

GradeMark – this is a tool within Turnitin that allows markers to add comments online www.help.turnitin.com/new-links.htm

Haines, C. 2004. *Assessing Students' Written Work: Marking Essays and Reports.* London: RoutledgeFalmer.

Using rubrics to improve marking reliability and to clarify good performance www.advance-he.ac.uk/knowledge-hub/using-rubrics-improve-marking-reliability-and-clarify-good-performance

Plagiarism detection

Turnitin: www.help.turnitin.com/new-links.htm

Chapter 7
Supporting students

[UKPSF: A4, V1, V2]

KEY FINDINGS FROM OUR SURVEY

Fifty-six per cent of respondents were *personal tutors*.
The main student-support challenges they faced were:

- Dealing with poor English-language skills of international students
- Knowing what to expect of students and understanding their previous educational experience
- Dealing with the diversity of students.

These issues were highlighted by a number of respondents. For example:

> The way we interact with students in my country is different to how it is done in the UK. Too much focus is made on negative aspects rather than praising the students for their achievements ... I had to adapt and change my own teaching philosophy, beliefs, and behaviour. It was a long path of trials and errors.
>
> French lecturer teaching in UK

> Getting students to trust me and interact.
>
> Italian lecturer working in the UK

> Finding it difficult to adopt to varying level of [students'] motivation and level.
>
> German lecturer teaching in Malaysia

The advice they offered:

> Don't hesitate to solicit help if you're feeling swamped, don't understand what's required of you, or are uncertain of what your students need.
>
> Canadian lecturer teaching in the UK

> To embrace [your] international identity and find ways to introduce it to the context of the course, for both self-confidence and effective communication/good connection with the students.
>
> Greek PhD student teaching in the UK

INTRODUCTION

UK universities are expected to provide students with the support they need to be successful in and benefit from higher education (HE) (QAA, 2018). The approach taken to student support is one of the distinctive features of UK HE and is very different to the approach taken in other countries so can be challenging for new international staff to understand. In this chapter, we shall start by looking at some models of student support and how these have developed. We will then look at what support is offered at different stages of the student's journey, by whom and how you might be expected to be involved. We conclude the chapter by looking at how you might support specific groups of students.

STUDENT-SUPPORT MODELS

Three models of student support were identified by Earwaker (1992).

- *Pastoral model*: a traditional approach to student support whereby academic staff provide academic and pastoral support. Usually manifested as a ***personal tutoring system*** where academic staff (personal tutors) provide advice and support to their allocated students. Seen as a reactive model as students often only engage when they need help.
- *Professional model*: professional, qualified staff, such as counsellors, are readily available to provide support to students. This support is separated from the student's academic course and the role of the academic is simply to refer students to the support units.

- *Curriculum model*: personal and academic support is embedded into the curriculum, often within specific modules. Students receive regular support and meetings with tutors whether they have a specific need or not, so this is seen as more developmental.

The pastoral model of tutoring has its origins in the tutorial system at Oxford and Cambridge universities, where students lived and studied within their college and had close relationships with tutors who provided academic and pastoral support (Earwaker, 1992). This model, of academic staff providing pastoral support, worked because student numbers were low and staff had regular contact with students individually or in small groups. However, as student numbers grew, issues arose with this model in relation to the workload it imposes on academics and a recognition that academics are not professionally trained to provide pastoral support. This resulted in a shift towards the use of a professional model with a growth in the development of central student-services units staffed by non-academic professional staff. These provide students with greater access to qualified support staff and are separate from the academic course, but this has led to issues around academic staff/student relationships and integration of students into HE (Thomas, 2006). To address the shortcomings of the previous models, Earwaker (1992) proposed the curriculum model, where support is integrated into the curriculum and ensures all students benefit from the support. This model grew in popularity in HE institutions (HEIs). However, the changing nature of the student population, with greater numbers, diversity and expectations of students, has resulted in HEIs needing to re-invent their approaches to student support to suit the needs of mass HE and the diversity of students (Wisker et al., 2008).

A number of HEIs are now adopting a blended model of student support as recommended by Lochtie et al. (2018) which brings together academic tutoring within the curriculum, personal tutoring and **professional support services** to provide a holistic approach to student support (see Figure 7.1). An additional layer of senior or enhanced personal tutors is recommended to enhance the link between personal tutoring and professional services (Lochtie et al., 2018).

The type of support that students need will vary as they journey into, through and out of university. This journey is often described as the *student lifecycle*. In this chapter we shall look at four stages of this lifecycle: pre-entry, induction, on-course and onwards progression. Table 7.1 identifies the type of support typically offered at these stages, who provides it

SUPPORTING STUDENTS

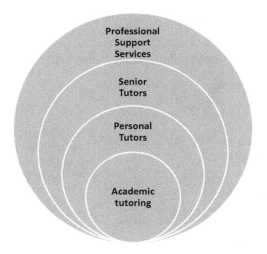

FIGURE 7.1 Blended model of student support
(adapted from McIntosh in Lochtie et al., 2018)

and what your role might be. We then expand on each of these stages in the following sections to explore this more fully.

PRE-ENTRY GUIDANCE

Students will receive a variety of information before they actually turn up at the university. This often includes practical information about accommodation, online registration, student cards, their IT account and paying fees but also aims to ensure students are ready for their academic course. A study of what works in terms of student retention (Thomas, 2012, p.22) suggests that the most effective pre-entry interventions combine the following roles:

- Providing information
- Informing expectations
- Developing academic skills
- Building social capital (links with peers, current students and staff)
- Nurturing a sense of belonging.

TABLE 7.1 Support required through the student lifecycle, and implications for teachers

Stage	Type of support	Provided by	Implications for teachers
Pre-entry	Information	University and school/department	
	Academic preparation	University and school/department	Be aware of what is done by whom. If you are a personal tutor, you may be expected to email your tutees before they arrive.
	Social capital	School, personal tutors, other students	
Induction	University induction	Professional services staff	
	School/department induction	Senior staff in school/department	Ensure you know the induction programme for new and returning students and what input, if any, you are expected to make. Often personal tutors meet their tutees during induction.
	Course induction	Course leader, personal tutors	
	Extra-curricular opportunities	Students' union personnel	
In-course	University specialist support	Professional services staff	Be aware of what's available and how to support students to access it.
	School/department support	Senior tutor and personal tutors	Familiarise yourself with policies regarding personal tutoring, office hours, etc.
	Academic support	Teaching staff	
Progression onwards	Graduation preparation	Graduation staff and alumni teams	Attend graduation!
	Careers advice and academic progression	Careers services staff and academics	Be aware of career and academic options.

Pre-entry support from teaching staff can include sharing some more information about the course, general guidance or an initial reading. At some institutions, personal tutors are expected to make contact with students by email before they arrive. Social media is being used increasingly to connect with students on the same course or in halls of residence together and create a sense of belonging even before students physically arrive on campus. Student buddying systems are also being used, where a new student is linked up to an existing student who acts as their buddy and provides advice and support. There may also be guidance and support for specific groups of students, such as international students or students with a disability, but more about that later.

INDUCTION

Students come to university at different stages of their life, with different educational backgrounds and expectations of HE. Some come straight from school or college, some after a year out from education, and others come from work, unemployment or caring roles. The transition into HE may be a challenging one both academically and socially, and teaching staff can play an important role in supporting students during this transition. Teaching staff are inevitably more focused on the academic transition; however, a survey of three institutions showed that whilst 70% of new students were confident that they could succeed in their course, 75% were concerned about making friends (Thomas, 2012). If students do not settle in to university socially then they may leave even if they like the course they have started, which impacts on university retention rates and finances.

To help students cope with this transition most institutions in the UK have traditionally run an *induction*, orientation or welcome event (often lasting a week) before the teaching of courses starts. *Induction* literally means "lead in", so it makes sense to lead students into university life. Induction weeks are used to orient students to being at university and typically include a range of activities, such as:

- *General university induction*: university registration, introduction to IT, library visits/talks, introduction to student services, health centre registration, etc.
- *School and course induction*: sessions delivered by the academic school, such as introduction to the school, introduction to the course, personal tutor meeting, welcome social events to get to meet staff and other students, etc.

- *Students' union activities*: most students' unions run a series of social events for new students, often called *Fresher's week*. As part of this, there is normally some sort of fair where new students have the opportunity to join any clubs or societies they are interested in.

The effectiveness of induction weeks was questioned due to the amount of information students were receiving passively in an intensive period (Edward, 2003). Current induction weeks tend to put more emphasis on subject-related activities and socialisation and minimise the information delivery sessions or spread them out over several weeks. There is also greater emphasis on the wider concept of student transition, which includes consideration of pre-entry guidance, induction and the whole first-year experience to help students transition from their previous educational or work setting to HE.

IN-COURSE SUPPORT

The blended model for student support identifies four key elements: academic tutoring, personal tutoring, **senior tutors** and professional services. Academic tutoring takes place within the curriculum so we shall focus here on the other elements of the blended model.

Personal tutoring

Personal tutoring is a key element of student support in UK HE (Yale, 2019) and has seen renewed interest in recent years (Grey and Osborne, 2018). Personal tutoring schemes usually involve each student being allocated a personal tutor to support them throughout their period of study. Definitions of a personal tutor vary considerably; this one from Stork and Walker (2015) includes both an academic and pastoral aspect of the role:

> A personal tutor is one who improves the intellectual and academic ability, and nurtures the emotional well-being of learners through individualised, holistic support.
>
> (p.9)

This definition falls into the traditional pastoral model of student support, but one of the things that differs between institutions is the extent to which the role is academic, pastoral or both. The terminology used to describe the role also varies; i.e. *personal tutor, academic tutor, academic advisor,* etc. For the purposes of this book we shall use *personal tutor.* Irrespective of the approach and terminology, it is likely that most new academic members of staff may be asked to fulfil some sort of tutoring role to support students. Non-academic members of staff may also be involved in this type of role, but it would be highly unusual for postgraduate students to be asked to be personal tutors for other students.

Most HEIs will have some sort of personal tutoring policy, which sets out their approach to supporting students, and written or online guidance for staff and students. However, our survey suggests that new staff are not always made aware of these during their staff induction. So, if you are expected to be a personal tutor, it is worth finding out the answers to the following questions:

- Is there a personal tutoring policy and/or guidelines?
- What type of support is available to new personal tutors; e.g. a briefing or course?
- What is the emphasis of the personal tutoring role: academic, pastoral, developmental?
- Do students normally have the same personal tutor for the duration of their degree, or do others take on aspects of this role at different stages; e.g. year tutors or dissertation supervisors?
- How many students are personal tutors usually responsible for and how is the workload for this allocated?
- What information are students given about what to expect and how is it provided?
- Are there any discrepancies between the written guidelines and what happens in practice?
- Is there someone in your school/department who is responsible for personal tutoring; e.g. a personal tutoring co-ordinator or senior tutor who can support you in this role?

(Based on Wisker et al., 2008)

Role of the personal tutor

Personal tutors support students through the transition into HE, progression through their course and onto the next step in their education or career. Given the various ways in which personal tutoring is conceived it is not surprising that the specific roles and responsibilities of a personal tutor vary. The personal tutor role can include:

- Being the first point of contact
- Providing information about HE processes, procedures and expectations
- Offering academic support and development
- Enhancing employability and personal development
- Providing personal welfare support
- Referring students to further information and support
- Identifying and responding to students at risk
- Creating a relationship that promotes a sense of belonging.

(Drawn from Lochtie et al., 2018; Thomas, 2006, 2012)

It is likely that you will be expected to keep some sort of record of your meetings, such as the date, issues discussed and agreed actions, but it is important not to record specific personal information. This may seem a daunting list for personal tutors, especially for those completely new to UK HE, so it is important to draw on any advice, guidance and training available from your institution and colleagues.

Personal tutoring challenges

Whilst personal tutoring can be a very rewarding experience, it can also be very challenging, especially for new staff. The following list of challenges has been developed from a personal tutoring workshop delivered at the University of Nottingham.

- *Role clarity*: even if the role and responsibilities are clearly laid out in a policy, there are often implicit assumptions about what personal tutors should and shouldn't do. It can be very difficult for staff new to the UK to get a sense of these until they have gained more experience of UK HE.
- *Inadequate training*: the written guidelines, support for and training of personal tutors has improved considerably in recent years and the introduction of senior tutors has really helped with this. However, practice is variable so if you have not been given advice then ask your colleagues the questions set out above.
- *Time needed*: balancing the demands of the personal tutoring role with other commitments is a considerable challenge. University

policies usually set out the minimum number and duration of meetings each year; however, dealing with certain tutees can take up a lot more time.

- *Academic regulations*: as a personal tutor you need to advise students about regulations around assessments, late submissions, extenuating circumstances and various other academic rules and regulations. These do vary at each university, so getting familiar with these can take time and experience.
- *Lack of engagement*: some students do not feel they need a personal tutor so don't engage unless they have a problem. If the personal tutoring role includes advice on study skills, employability, etc., then students are more likely to value the personal tutor meeting (Tryfona et al., 2013).
- *Setting boundaries*: part of the personal tutor role is to establish a relationship with your tutees, but watch out for students becoming over-familiar or over-dependent. Do not give out your personal contact details to tutees. Try and protect yourself and your time by not taking on extra tutees and by sticking to meeting times.
- *Offering support versus encouraging independence*: it can be difficult to find the right balance between supporting students and developing independent learners, which is one of the aims of HE. Try not to get drawn into trying to solve tutees' problems for them; instead support them to resolve problems and face challenges themselves.
- *Students' personal problems*: it is very likely that at some stage a student will turn to you for support in dealing with what can be very personal problems, and you may feel ill-equipped to advise them. It is really important that you do not give advice on issues that are outside your expertise as an academic; i.e. mental health, medical advice, etc. The legal advice is that if a member of staff provides advice and this goes wrong they will be judged as that of a trained counsellor rather than a well-meaning academic (Hughes et al., 2018).
- *Referral process*: it can be difficult to decide at what point you should refer a student on to professional services for advice. Given the increase in mental health issues of young people in UK HE, many institutions now have specific publications and/or websites for all staff to guide them.

For an example, see the University of Nottingham's Identifying and Responding to Students in Difficulty guide for staff in *Further resources*.

Many of the challenges above emanate from a disjoint between staff and student expectations of the personal tutoring process. To help manage expectations it is advisable to discuss expectations, establish ground rules and agree responsibilities regarding note-taking at the start. The first meeting with personal tutees is a good time to do this.

Confidentiality claims

It is really important to be aware of your institution's approach to the confidentiality of personal tutoring meetings and discuss these with tutees from the outset. Whilst some claim that personal tutor meetings are confidential, others make it clear that personal tutors are not bound by confidentiality in the same way as medical and counselling staff are. When dealing with a particular student issue, personal tutors need to be able to consult relevant colleagues such as the senior tutors or specialist support staff, but this can often be done without the student's name being shared. So whilst all personal tutors should treat the information shared by tutees sensitively, the expectations around limits of confidentiality will vary. If, however, a student declares information that means they or someone else is at risk then confidentiality is over-ridden by a duty of care and the information should be passed onto the relevant professional services.

Sometimes concerned parents will contact members of staff. Under UK data-protection rules staff at HEIs are not allowed to disclose personal information to anyone outside the university, so it is really important that you familiarise yourself with your university's policy on confidentiality and record-keeping.

Personal tutoring outside the UK

For staff working in UK HE outside the UK, personal tutoring has the added complexity that it is carried out within a different country with its own laws, norms and expectations. So, for instance, in some countries there is an expectation that the university will act *in loco parentis* — i.e. in place of the parent — and therefore parents expect to be able to discuss their child's progress with university staff. As explained above, this is not permitted under the UK data-protection rules. As a result, new staff can feel torn between two systems and unsure how this should influence their practice. It is the institution's responsibility in establishing its provision outside the UK to consider the implications of any conflicts between standard UK university practice and the host country's laws and practices. These are likely to be addressed via student-registration procedures when students agree to the institution's terms and conditions. So the advice for staff is to follow the rules as set out by the institution that you work for. In the event that there is an issue then the institution would be held accountable rather than the individual member of staff.

Personal tutoring plays an important role in most UK universities and most teaching staff are likely to be involved in this role at some stage. This area has seen renewed interest in recent years, not least because three of the questions on the National Student Survey (NSS, 2019) are around the academic support given to students:

12. I have been able to contact staff when I needed to.
13. I have received sufficient advice and guidance in relation to my course.
14. Good advice was available when I needed to make study choices on my course.

Senior tutors

To enhance the personal tutoring system, a number of universities introduced a network of senior personal tutors or academic co-ordinators that operate at university, faculty or school level; e.g. the University of Nottingham introduced senior tutors in 2003. Again the approach will differ at each university but they generally form a pyramid, with a university senior tutor overseeing the work of senior tutors in each school/department who oversee the work of personal tutors in their school (see Figure 7.2). The university-level senior tutor tends to have overall responsibility for all aspects of personal tutoring at the university, including policy, guidance, training, co-ordinating and supporting school senior tutors, and provides a link between academic schools and professional services. School-level senior tutors support personal tutors in their school, provide advice and guidance, ensure new personal tutors have an appropriate induction, and make sure all students are allocated a personal tutor and know what support they can provide. This enhanced network of tutoring is designed to ensure that personal tutors receive more support and training, and students better understand the role of the personal tutor and feel supported by the university.

FIGURE 7.2 An example of a senior tutor network

Professional support services

Each university will have a range of professional support services available to students and staff. Some of these are focused on supporting students and staff in their day-to-day living and provide accommodation, medical centres, mental health support, counselling service, finance advice, childcare, faith centres, sport and recreation facilities, arts centres, etc. Others are more specifically focused on helping students be successful in their academic studies:

- Student service centres
- Library and learning centres
- Academic skills support
- IT support
- Careers.

Others provide support for specific groups of students such as students with a disability or international students, and we shall discuss these later. Most of these services will offer a variety of opportunities for students to get support, such as drop-in sessions, individual advice, workshops and online advice or courses. This support can also be integrated into academic courses as per the curriculum model of student support outlined earlier. Often professional services staff are invited to have some input into courses and modules at relevant points, such as induction or final-year preparation for careers.

The structure and organisation of professional services varies from one institution to the next, with some services provided centrally and others located in each campus or each faculty. Many institutions hold a welcome event for new staff where these services advertise their role in the university. These can be a good way to find out what services are available for staff and for students to be referred to at appropriate points.

According to Thomas (2012), professional services provide a vital role for some students but many students do not know what is available or do not engage. The majority of those thinking of leaving seek advice from friends and family rather than professional services. Students are more likely to engage with professional services if:

- They are easily accessible
- Students feel they need to engage
- They are located within the academic sphere (i.e. schools or departments)
- They adopt a more holistic approach of study advice and personal development (as opposed to a deficit model)
- There is good communication between services.

(Based on Thomas, 2012)

When students engage with professional services they get advice from qualified staff whose roles are dedicated to supporting students. However, Hughes et al. (2018) caution that if professional services do not provide the support students need, or demand on the services is too high, students will turn to academics for support, which can put the academic at risk of providing advice in areas beyond their expertise. One of the quotes from a survey respondent illustrates that the system does not always work as effectively as it should:

I would have and still would appreciate having a student services support team that had the capacity to support students in a timely manner.
Irish/American teaching fellow teaching in UK

So whilst professional services provide an important role in supporting students at university, there are challenges in terms of their capacity, getting students to engage and ensuring academics refer students to the appropriate service.

Students' union

Most UK HEIs have a students' union that also provides support for students, such as advice on courses, housing, employment, money, health and well-being as well as organising social activities. Whilst these tend to

SUPPORTING STUDENTS

operate independently of the university it is useful to know what is available so you can advise students that they can get support there.

PROGRESSION ONWARDS

After their degree, many students will want to find a job or go on to further study. The point at which students start to think about their next steps varies. Some will have specifically chosen a degree course that has a work placement, so they have already started thinking about this before they arrive. Others will not give this much thought until their final year. Careers services usually provide advice on writing CVs, job applications and interview skills and can help students identify what careers they could pursue. Many universities run careers fairs, where employers come to the university to advertise their company and recruit potential employees. Sometimes there will be specific sessions organised as part of courses or modules that relate to future opportunities. These may be guest speakers from industry or talks about what future study opportunities there are for students.

On completion of their course, students who pass are eligible to graduate, and this is one of the highlights of the academic year. This is the culmination of a student's course and is a special time for them, their families and friends. Academic staff are normally expected to attend graduation and it is a lovely opportunity to mingle with the students and celebrate this achievement with them.

SUPPORTING SPECIFIC STUDENTS

As mentioned above, some of the professional services at HEIs are aimed at groups of students that may need specific support to ensure they can fully engage in their studies. This includes students with a disability, international students and those that are under-represented in UK HE. Here we discuss the support needs of some of these groups of students and the types of support available. It is worth finding out what support service units there are at your institutions as they usually provide advice for staff as well as students.

International and transnational education students

In 2018/19, 20% of students studying in UK HEIs were international students, making up 485,000 of the 2.38 million students (HESA, 2020). As well as the usual transition issues discussed above, international students face additional challenges in their transition into UK HE which have been categorised as:

- *Culture shock*: adjusting to the different environment, customs and practices of the UK.
- *Language shock*: even though international students have to have a certain proficiency in English to get into UK universities, this does not always prepare them adequately for conversing in everyday conversations and academic discussions. Even native English speakers may find it difficult to adjust to the local accents, speed of speech and conversation.
- *Academic shock*: in addition to the academic shock for UK students coming from school, prior educational experiences, customs and ways of behaving are often very different to the UK approach.

(Based on Ryan, 2005)

Most universities run separate induction sessions for international students either prior to the main student induction week or as part of it. These typically include advice on visas, police registration, safety, finance, health, transport and adjusting to living in the country, to help with culture shock. There may also be academic-related sessions to help students understand the approach to UK HE. Pre-entry English-language support is normally available to assist with the language.

The latest figures on transnational education (TNE) in the UK gathered in 2016/17 showed that 85% of UK universities were involved in delivering TNE, involving over 707,000 students (Universities UK International, 2018). Many of these students will be classed as home students (as they live in the country where the course is delivered) and others will be classed as international students. The home TNE students will not face the same culture shock as international students but are likely to still experience language and academic shock.

Non-native English speakers

One of the main student-support issues raised by new international staff in our surveys was around the English-language proficiency of their students.

> I realised that a lot of international students do not have the level of English required to follow a HE program in the UK – should I lower my speed/content etc. so that the international students

SUPPORTING STUDENTS

could follow ... or let the international students not understand what is going on? The university has clearly a role to play here in admitting students with the appropriate level of English otherwise other students might suffer from it.

French PhD student teaching in UK

Understanding the requirements and abilities of predominately non-native English speaking student cohorts.

Irish/American lecturer teaching in China

In order to be accepted onto a degree course in the UK, international or TNE students whose first language is not English have to demonstrate that their English-language skills are sufficient to be able to study for their degree. There are various ways they can do this, including passing an in-house course or test set by the institution. One common way is to obtain an International English Language Testing System (IELTS) score. The test assesses four skills: reading, writing, speaking and listening, each scored from 0–9. To gain a Tier 4 student visa to study in the UK, students need a score of 4.0 overall and in each skill for below degree level or pre-sessional courses (courses attended before starting the main course of study). For degree courses and above, students need a score of 5.5 overall and in each of the four skills to obtain a visa. However, the English-language requirements required to study at degree level or higher are set by each institution for its courses. As a result, most UK HEIs offer some type of pre-sessional English for Academic Purposes course for international students who need to improve their English-language skills before commencing their degree. The duration of these will vary depending on the individual's current skill. Generally, those who have attended a pre-sessional English course do not need to attend the induction sessions for international students as they will already have covered the information, but this will vary so it is worth checking.

Students studying at UK HEIs outside the UK do not need a UK visa but are still likely to be able to demonstrate their English-language skills or attend a course prior to starting their degree. Given that the majority of students may not speak English as their first language, there may be a foundation year of English-language and study skills tuition for students before they commence their undergraduate degree.

Widening participation (or access) for students

In Chapter 1 we discussed how HEIs have **widening participation** (WP) initiatives (*widening access* in Scotland) initiatives aimed at increasing the proportion of students in UK HE that come from under-represented groups such as people with disabilities, lower-income families and some ethnic minorities. Most institutions have WP teams within their professional services whose role is to ensure better access, success and progression for these students. They usually liaise with local schools and run open days, taster days and summer schools to give students from those groups the opportunity to experience university life. As teaching staff, you may be asked to contribute to some of these events.

Many universities now use contextual information about applicants' educational and socio-economic background to give applicants from disadvantaged backgrounds a slightly lower offer for grades needed for admission. In Scotland, from 2020 universities will publicise the standard grade offer and a minimum offer, which is only available to widening-access students.

Even if you are not involved directly in WP events you need to be aware of some of the issues that impact on students from a WP background. Recent statistics reveal some really concerning trends around the progression of some of these students, with one report showing that 79.6% of white UK-domiciled students gained a first or 2:1 degree whereas only 55.5% of black students did so (Advance HE, 2018a) despite having the same entry qualifications. This attainment gap is a major focus for much of the equality, diversity and inclusion work currently going on in UK universities. As a result, staff are being encouraged to adopt inclusive teaching practices which enable all students to take part in learning and fulfil their potential, by removing any barriers that prevent students from learning.

Students with a disability

The number of students with a declared disability has been growing year on year, with an increase in mental health conditions being the main cause. In 2018/19 13.9% of students (approximately 331,000) in UK HE declared a disability. Of these 36% were in the category of *specific learning difficulty*, which is just under 120,000 students (HESA, 2020).

When students apply to a university in the UK, they are asked if they have a disability, and if so they are usually referred to the professional service that supports students with a disability, often called *disability services* or *enabling services*. These staff will then get in touch with the student to assess their needs and put a plan in place to ensure the student is able to engage fully with their course when they arrive. There are various ways in which teachers will be alerted to the fact that they are teaching a student with a disability. Sometimes this is through a school disability liaison officer, or increasingly this information is available on student-record systems. The support plan will outline what support the student needs to be able to participate fully. This might include getting lecture notes in advance, having extra time for assessment or in exams, using a computer instead of writing in exams, having a note-taker in lectures, etc. Increasingly there is an expectation that we develop inclusive practices in teaching, learning and assessment so that the need for reasonable adjustments is diminished.

 FURTHER RESOURCES

Pre-entry and induction

Induction resource from Advance HE
www.advance-he.ac.uk/knowledge-hub/induction
O'Donnell, V.L., Kean, M., and Stevens, G. 2016. *Student Transition in Higher Education*. York: Higher Education Academy
www.heacademy.ac.uk/system/files/downloads/student_transition_in_higher_education.pdf

Personal tutoring

Lochtie, D., McIntosh, E., Stork, A., and Walker, B. 2018. *Effective Personal Tutoring in Higher Education*. St Albans: Critical Publishing.
Examines the role of the personal tutor in HE in depth and provides lots of advice for personal tutors on skills required, setting boundaries, support through the student lifecycle and coaching.
University of Newcastle Senior Tutor Role Description
www.ncl.ac.uk/ltds/assets/documents/qsh-personaltutoring-st-role.pdf
Thomas, L., andHixenbaugh, P. 2006. *Personal Tutoring in Higher Education*. London: Institute of Education Press. Chapter 3: Widening Participation and the Increased Need for Personal Tutoring.
University of Nottingham Identifying and Responding to Students in Difficulty guide for staff
www.nottingham.ac.uk/counselling/documents/identifying-and-responding-to-students-in-difficulty.pdf

International students

Carroll, J., Ryan, J., and Ryan, J. 2005. *Teaching International Students: Improving Learning for All*. London: Routledge.
Explores the challenges of teaching international students and provides lots of useful advice from practitioners to help ensure a more positive learning environments for international students in the HE system.

Scudamore, R. 2013. *Engaging Home and International Students: A Guide for New Lecturers*. HEA
www.advance-he.ac.uk/knowledge-hub/engaging-home-and-international-students-guide-new-lecturers

Study International website

Provides help and advice for international students www.studyinternational.com/

Teaching International Students Project

A range of resources were developed as part of this 2014 project by the Higher Education Academy to support lecturers and other teaching staff working with international students www.advance-he.ac.uk/knowledge-hub/teaching-international-students-project

UK Council for International Student Affairs

Supports international students and the institutions, students' unions and organisations who work closely with them
www.ukcisa.org.uk/

STUDENTS WITH A DISABILITY

Advance HE. 2018. *Equality in Higher Education: Statistical Report 2018*. A useful source for data on age, disability, ethnicity, gender and other characteristics of students in UK HE
www.advance-he.ac.uk/knowledge-hub/equality-higher-education-statistical-report-2018

Disability Rights UK
www.disabilityrightsuk.org/adjustments-disabled-students

Equality, Diversity and Inclusion section of Advance HE website
www.advance-he.ac.uk/guidance/equality-diversity-and-inclusion

Hughes, G., Panjwani, M., Priya, T., and Byrom, N. 2018. *Student Mental Health: The Role and Experiences of Academics*. Leeds: Student Minds.

WIDENING PARTICIPATION

Thomas, L. 2012. *Building Student Engagement and Belonging in Higher Education at a Time of Change: Final Report from the What Works? Student Retention & Success Programme*. London: Paul Hamlyn Foundation.

A report on a series of projects that looked at student retention and success rates. Provides useful guidance on pre-entry information, induction and on-going support of students.

www.advance-he.ac.uk/knowledge-hub/building-student-engagement-and-belonging-higher-education-time-change-final-report

Chapter 8

Ongoing development of your professional practice

[UKPSF: A5, K5 & V3]

KEY FINDINGS FROM OUR SURVEY

The most useful forms of support for new teachers were:

- Discussions with colleagues and mentors
- Teaching observation.

The least useful were:

- University induction
- School induction.

The main challenges they faced were:

- A lack of appropriate induction for their teaching role
- The support offered was not tailored for international staff.

In terms of what helps:

> Maybe having the time to watch other professors present their lectures. I think this opportunity would enhance my understanding of students' culture, behaviour, etc.
> Brazilian lecturer teaching in the UK

153

A mentor to ask specific questions about the module I'm leading and bureaucratic procedures.
Italian researcher teaching in China

Observe other teachers and enrol in the PGCHE [Postgraduate Certificate in Higher Education].
European lecturer teaching in the UK

Talk to colleagues as much as possible and find out all the little details about your department and how/when things happen.
Portuguese researcher teaching in the UK

Attend workshops/courses offered by the Uni even if they are not compulsory.
Chilean PhD teaching in the UK

INTRODUCTION

These are the three themes of this chapter:

1. How do you know that what you do is good enough (quality assurance)?
2. How can you get better (quality enhancement)?
3. Does quality get recognised?

The first reviews the different ways in which our courses are evaluated and asks you to think about how you will find out about the range of feedback that is available to you. It also looks at the other sources of evidence that you can collect and act on. The second, addressing the development aspect of the title of the chapter, asks you to think about: (1) what opportunities are out there to help you progress all aspects of your academic life and the teaching aspect of your role in particular; and (2) what is your plan (your continuing professional development, or CPD, plan) for the next few years that will help you get to your next career goal, be it tenure, promotion or the next job. The last looks at the ways in which you can gain recognition; be that by qualification, UK Professional Standards Framework (UKPSF) fellowship or teaching awards.

Before we start to think about the evidence that we can collect to give us a measure of the quality of what we do (who can tell us what?), it is worth taking a moment to define two terms. You will recall from the Dennis model

(Chapter 4) that the course-design process includes both assessment and evaluation. Generally in the UK we make the distinction that *assessment measures the learning* whilst *evaluation measures the teaching.* You may find in some articles and texts, particularly from countries other than the UK, that the two words are interchangeable. This slight confusion is added to as we talk about giving *feedback* in both cases; whilst in assessment the feedback is given to the learner, in evaluation the feedback is given to the teacher. This chapter, then, is about evaluation of practice and what we do with the results (the feedback, the metrics and the comments) in order to improve. With that in mind, let us return to the question: *Who* can tell us *what*? We will add *when?* to that list and a little bit of *how?* as we look at the possibilities.

HOW DO YOU KNOW THAT WHAT YOU DO IS GOOD ENOUGH (QUALITY ASSURANCE)?

Who to ask?

There are three possible sources of evidence, which is why some colleagues talk about **triangulation**.

1. *Students*: they can tell you about their experience of, and satisfaction/engagement with, the teaching and learning activities that you provide. As we detail below, there are a number of ways in which students *evaluate* courses at different stages of their degree course. Some are through questionnaires/surveys, some are by discussion (focus groups) and some by committee (staff–student committees at various levels in the institution, sometimes labelled the *student voice* or *student engagement*). The outcomes of student work – assessments, assignments and examinations – can also give indications; if they all pass with very high marks that tells us one thing, whilst if they all fail that tells us another. Also student choices (if they have any) can be indicative; is your module/unit very popular or does it struggle to attract applicants – what does that say to us? Lastly, many institutions now have student-led teaching awards, and your students may nominate you for recognition of good practice in one or more categories. We will look at awards and recognition in more detail later in this chapter, but for the moment simply flag that they are part of the landscape.
2. *Peers*: whilst students can indicate satisfaction and engagement with a course, they cannot comment on currency or accuracy which is

one possible role of peers. You need to think about what peers can best comment on and integrate that with how students report their experience of the same. There are a number of ways of learning from peers; for example:

- You may ask a colleague to comment on your plans for some lectures, tutorials, practical classes or assignments for currency, level and relevance.
- The external examiner may comment on your assessment/assignments and/or the quality of your grading and feedback and/or the marks awarded for your assessments.
- You might team teach and your colleague(s) observes your class and comments.
- You might ask an experienced colleague to review aspects of your face-to-face or online practice.
- You might be required to attend an early-career training course (more on that later) that includes review of your teaching by a peer on the course, or a peer in your discipline or a member of the course team.
- You could observe other colleagues teach or review their use of the virtual learning environment (VLE) as a means of finding aspects of practice that you could adopt (if good) or avoid (if less so).
- You could attend a learning circle or similar, where a group of colleagues meet to talk about researching and developing pedagogy and sharing good practice.

3. *You*: sometimes one can walk away from a class smiling and thinking that it went really well; both a head and heart response. On another occasion the reverse may be true; one feels disheartened and recognises a number of places where the class did not work. It is this personal review or reflection that give another insight into the quality of one's practice. This leads us into the concept of **reflective practice** and **reflective practitioner** that we will return to later.

Having identified the *who*, let us think about those three sources of evidence in turn, thinking more about the *what*, but always bearing in mind that we need to combine the views of all three (triangulation) if we are to make useful conclusions and so action-plan for change.

What (and when)?

Student surveys

It is not unusual for institutions to run multiple student surveys and in order to avoid further survey-fatigue individual staff are asked to refrain from implementing additional surveys themselves. As a result most of the feedback that we receive from students is through institutionally driven means. What you need to ensure is that you are able to gain the information that particularly applies to you and what you do. Let us look at some mainstream surveys to see what information they can tell us.

Module/unit survey (often termed something like *student evaluation of modules*, or SEMs): many places insist that this survey is taken each time the module/unit runs. Some higher education institutions (HEIs) have moved to a risk approach and only run the survey if the module/unit has been changed in a major way (for example, if teaching staff have changed or the assessment regime has been altered) or the last evaluation results were poor. The rationale is that if it seems to be running well then it is *not broken so no need to fix it*, and there is the hope that reducing the number of surveys completed by students may lead to them being more diligent in responding to those surveys that they are asked to complete. Invariably these surveys are standard and fixed and you cannot change or add to the questions asked. They are run by a central unit, and in some places the results are published, and your part is solely to read the outcomes and act on them. The sorts of questions included give metrics and comments. Likert-scale (rating) questions generate the numbers and open questions produce the words.

Students may be asked to give feedback on their experience of: resources, both availability and quality; workload; assessment and feedback (to them) processes; clarity of expectations (learning outcomes), etc. Typically these are satisfaction surveys and would be more valuable if there were some questions about engagement; what the students did. If you are only one of the teachers on a module/unit – team teaching – it can sometimes be difficult to untangle the messages and gain individual feedback, but it is important that you discuss outcomes with others and decide what, if anything, needs to change. Usually, institutions expect module/unit leaders to write a report in response to the data collected that shows plans for the future, and you should to be part of this discussion.

Staff teaching survey (often termed something like *student evaluation of teaching*, or SETs): some institutions run surveys enabling students to give feedback to individual members of staff at the end of a module/unit.

These are usually satisfaction surveys and give views on the teaching and teacher. As with SEMs above, the sorts of questions included give metrics and comments. Obviously these can be very useful sources of data as they refer directly to you. It can also be helpful to look at the metrics pertaining to other staff as this allows you to benchmark yourself. If you score an average of 3.5/5 then that might or might not be grounds for celebration. However, if everyone else averages 3.0/5 that tells you that ... but if the average of others is 4.5/5 that tells another story. There is ongoing review and questions about the value of student evaluation – see Hornstein and Law (2017), for example. However, they are an accepted and acceptable part of the evidence base that we can gather and should be read in conjunction with all other forms of data.

Year satisfaction survey: when the National Student Survey (NSS; see Chapter 1 and the next item in this list) was introduced, some institutions started to use the same or similar questions to gain feedback at the end of Year 1 and/or Year 2 of the course. This means that any issues or concerns are spotted earlier and measures put in place to respond to them. Invariably this improves the NSS scores when that survey is taken. Year surveys tend to focus on big-picture questions and may give little in terms of individual teacher feedback. However, they can be very useful to illuminate trends across a year or highlight perceived major weaknesses.

NSS (www.thestudentsurvey.com): as mentioned in Chapter 1, this survey is run by an external agency and all final-year undergraduate students have the opportunity to feed back on their experiences of their whole degree course. As the results of this survey are made public it is very useful to know what the graduating students are saying, but again you may find that it is more big-picture outcomes than individual feedback. However, the messages are always worth hearing and responding to. In *Further resources* we have added links to the standard questions and more details of the process.

Postgraduate Taught Experience Survey (PTES): again this annual survey is run externally to institutions; in this case Advance HE invites taught postgraduate students to give feedback on their experiences of their course. The outcomes are made public and, as Advance HE says, aggregated results from all participating institutions provide a comprehensive picture of the postgraduate taught experience. There is an equivalent for research students – the Postgraduate Research Experience Survey (PRES) – which can be used to gather information about the experience of any research student on a doctoral or research master's course. See *Further resources* for links to the surveys.

Graduate Outcomes Survey: run annually by the Higher Education Statistics Agency, it invites graduates, one year after graduation, to give feedback on how well their course prepared them for the workplace. Again a big-picture survey but very helpful when reviewing the overall composition of a degree course. If your graduates tell you that they feel unprepared for aspects of the workplace then they are very important messages and will need addressing across the degree course.

The International Student Barometer (ISB): an online questionnaire run by I-Graduate with feedback from over 3 million students worldwide, across all levels and years of study, the ISB claims to be the leading benchmarking tool for the international student experience. See *Further resources* for links.

You will need to check which surveys are in place where you are and how you can find out the results and so contribute to discussion of and responses to the outcomes. You also need to check which surveys give feedback that is relevant to you, and decide how you will respond to the messages they contain, taking account of the views of peers and your own reflections too.

Whilst we are listing which information we gain from student surveys, at different stages of their course, it is worth spending a few moments considering other ways that we can gain students' views.

1. *Individual students: focus groups.* One concern with surveys is that the result may indicate an issue but not provide sufficient detail to help formulate a response. In this instance you may wish to get a small number of students together and ask focused questions (a focus group) in order to dig a little deeper. It may be more productive if you get a colleague to do this on your behalf as students may not be willing to be totally open when face-to-face with the person who may be marking their work.
2. *Individual students: interim evaluation.* You will have noticed that the surveys listed above are completed after teaching and learning is finished: at the end of the module/unit, the end of the year, the end of the degree, after they have left the institution. This means that any response you make can improve things for the next cohort(s), and explains why this section is headed *What (and when)?* Many of us, however, want to respond to concerns of the cohort who are in front of us, our current students, and make timely changes if we can. It is worth considering, say half-way through the module/unit, asking a few questions about topics that you know you can respond to if there are concerns. For example:

    ■ Resources – what is available in the VLE and library – you can act quickly to change the situation

159

- Clarity of expectations – you cannot change the learning outcomes (a major change in course-design terms; see Chapter 4) but you could spend a little more time explaining and illustrating what they mean at the start of classes
- Understanding of how they will be assessed and what the assessment criteria mean – again, spending some more time giving a better insight and, maybe, some examples (also see Chapter 6).

This sort of interim evaluation can be done, anonymously, in one of several ways:

- Using electronic voting systems of the type we use in lectures (Top Hat, TurningPoint, etc.)
- Sticky notes on the back wall as they leave the room: red ones for concerns and blue ones for things that are working well
- A brief email or VLE survey (notice the *brief* if you want quantity as well as quality answers). One way is to ask three questions: What should I carry on doing/stop doing/start doing?
- A show of hands in a large-group setting in response to some clear questions – relatively anonymous and quick to do and avoids using the technology
- The one-minute paper (Lightbody and Nicholl, 2013, and Stead, 2005) is a written task, which is designed to take learners one minute or less to answer, that prompts students to reflect on the class and give feedback. By careful selection of the question, you can gain feedback on a range of aspects:

   □ What questions do you have about today's concepts/topics?
   □ Was there an idea discussed in today's class that you disagree with or concerns you?
   □ How does today's class link with our last two lectures and workshops?
   □ Where would you place yourself against today's intended learning outcomes?

See *Further resources* for more ideas about the one-minute paper and good practice from Seattle University.

Interim evaluation is all about quickly gaining indications of how things are going and should not be long and complex; colleagues often talk about 'quick and dirty' methods because they are hardly scientific but they do get the messages you need in a fast and timely manner.

ONGOING DEVELOPMENT

3. *Student representation.* Most courses have staff–student committees or advisory groups (the names vary but the purpose is the same, namely to include students in discussions and decision making). These may be organised at the year or whole-course level, or both, and tend to focus more on big-picture issues rather than providing individual feedback to a member of staff; but they could go into details if necessary. We mention them here as they are part of the evidence that may be useful to you in building up a picture of whether what you are doing is working well or not (benchmarking against other peers involved on the course) and be a place for you to hear about what is working well (or not) elsewhere on the course, so alerting you to good practice and colleagues who you might wish to talk to and learn from. Students are represented on most university committees (student voice/engagement) and students' unions both locally and nationally play an important part in training representatives. In *Further resources* we have included some useful links to the National Union of Students (NUS) and Advance HE concerning the student voice.

A final comment on student surveys before we move on. You will have noticed that surveys have been labelled as *satisfaction* (happiness) or *engagement* (involved) surveys; some attempt both. At the time of writing there is considerable discussion about this in the UK and a move to include more in terms of engagement – what the student contributes to the partnership of teaching/learning – questions. In the United States there is an engagement survey available for institutions (see *Further resources* for the National Survey of Student Engagement) and the NSS in the UK has, after 10 years of the same (satisfaction-led) questions, changed to include aspects of engagement. We need to recognise that this is a partnership and students are responsible for their learning in the same way we are responsible for their teaching.

We have talked about *who* we can ask for evidence and *what* sorts of evidence are usually readily available to us. In passing we have noted *when* we can and could collect the data, and spent a little time on the *how* to collect, but there is nothing on the *why*. For more on the latter two we suggest Butcher et al. (2020) in this series of texts (see chapter 11 in particular).

Before moving to the second theme of this chapter – getting better – it is worth thinking about how you might collate and deal with the information that is collected. Some institutions, but not all, expect their staff to compile a teaching portfolio (physical or electronic) which is then used for tenure, promotion and award applications. The portfolio will include the data (probably as annexes) and a narrative that considers the various sources – *reflection* – and then decisions on what to do – an *action plan*. As noted above, it is usual for groups teaching a course to review the feedback and action plan; this could add to your evidence base. We have included a range of ideas and resources about portfolios in *Further resources*. If you are not required to create a portfolio, we recommend that you establish some way of collecting and collating this sort of information. There will be times when you want to use abstracts at least from this data for applications: probation, tenure, promotion, reward payments, your next post, awards. It is really helpful at those times to have the evidence (metrics, student quotes, commendations, peer quotes, peer-observation outcomes, head-of-department references, etc.) readily available, collated and summarised and not in a heap in the corner of the office! One difficulty, as an early-career academic, is benchmarking the data, and this is one of the values of triangulation; comparing and contrasting information from different sources enables you to put some of the more positive and negative feedback in context and helps ground your decisions and planned actions. Whatever, it is worth discussing your thinking with a mentor (more on this later) or colleague who you trust to act as a critical friend; someone who agrees to speak honestly and openly, but constructively, about weaknesses, problems and issues.

HOW CAN YOU GET BETTER (QUALITY ENHANCEMENT)?

Developing practice

There are a number of ways available to staff in universities to develop their practice, and you should check to see what will be helpful to you, remembering what the respondents to our survey said at the start of this chapter.

1. *Institutional provision*:
    a. Early-career staff may be required, or can opt, to register for an initial training course related to teaching and managing student learning in HE. There are a variety of these available; some online and some based on workshops. Some result in a qualification, usually a postgraduate certificate (60 credits at master's level). Some are accredited by Advance HE for

ONGOING DEVELOPMENT

recognition of a UKPSF fellowship and some are accredited against the Staff and Educational Development Association Professional Development Framework (SEDA PDF). There is more about the UKPSF and SEDA PDF below, but at this stage it is worth noting that many institutions now require staff to gain at least Descriptor 2 (Fellow status) of the UKPSF scheme or a postgraduate HE teaching qualification as part of their probationary requirement.

b. Most institutions have a staff/academic-development unit or centre (the names vary but their missions are similar) that offers resources and a range of short training courses in all aspects of academic work, including learning and teaching. Some are based around workshops whilst others are online. Colleagues in these units/centres will be able to point you to a range of both institutional and external development opportunities, and they should be your first port of call.

c. Some universities are establishing academies or centres of teaching excellence (see *Further resources* for some examples) that aim to build on early-career development and provide a range of collegial opportunities to enhance teaching and learning within a particular context/mission. Learning circles – a way of organising, sharing and recognising the collective wisdom of a group – are a prime example of this, as demonstrated by the Warwick International Higher Education Academy (WIHEA) at the University of Warwick.

d. Many institutions promote peer review/observation (Fullerton, 2003, and Hammersley-Fletcher and Orsmond, 2004). The schemes and focus vary but the basic idea is that we can learn from peers. Some focus on observing live teaching; sitting in the room whilst a colleague teaches and then discussing the experience afterwards as a means of both gaining ideas and feedback. Others focus more widely and a peer may look, say, at your online materials or your assessment and feedback methods and discuss their thoughts and observations with you. See *Further resources* (peer observation) for the example of the Teaching and Learning Observation College (TLOC) at the University of Nottingham as an institutional approach to this, and other useful links and details (peer review).

e. Some institutions offer opportunities to gain ***360-degree feedback*** – these schemes enable multiple raters – such as mentors, supervisors, peers, direct reports, subordinates and

ONGOING DEVELOPMENT

        external peers – to leave feedback on you. The feedback is then used as a benchmark within your development plan.

    f. Some HEIs have developed massive online open courses (MOOCs) that address this topic – see *Further resources* for the online MOOC from the University of New South Wales (UNSW Sydney).

2. *Disciplinary groups*:

    a. Your school/department may organise away days to focus on a particular topic or topics in order to ensure that good practice is shared or all are following a particular approach.

    b. Some schools/departments have pedagogy or education research groups or learning circles that provide a collegial space to develop practice by sharing and researching.

    c. Most disciplines have a professional body associated with them, and these often have education groups that offer opportunities – meetings, conferences, networks, publications – to share and develop practice within the discipline.

3. *National groups*:

    a. Advance HE says it supports "transformative leadership and management, teaching and learning, equality, diversity and inclusion and effective governance" (www.advance-he.ac.uk) and offers online resources, networks (some of which are disciplinary) and conferences.

    b. As noted above, there are professional/disciplinary groups that you will know of or colleagues will be able to advise you about.

4. *Literature/published scholarship in learning and teaching*:

    a. You have started down this road already as you are reading this text and we are directing you to a range of other publications in the *Further resources* sections of the book.

    b. If you take any course leading to a qualification or apply for recognition against the UKPSF, you will need to refer to the literature on learning and teaching. Some courses include a small project where you research an aspect of your own teaching and, again, you will need to check what others say in the scholarship on learning and teaching in your discipline.

    c. There are some useful learning and teaching newsletters that summarise ideas and point you to further research and

ONGOING DEVELOPMENT

literature. *Tomorrow's Professor* is a good example; see *Further resources* for more.

5. *Reflective practice/reflective practitioner*: many approaches to self-development are based on the concept of reflective practice (Schön, 1983); reflection is about transforming experience into learning. After a class or meeting with students you pause to think about how that went. You may draw on several forms of the evidence that we have outlined above in this review of your experience, and as a result you make judgements about the quality, effectiveness or appropriateness, etc. Then you start thinking about how the class or meeting could be improved next time, which may require you to draw on additional evidence (scholarship, conversations with peers), which is called action planning. Part of your planning might be that you need to know more or learn something new – which leads us into CPD (see below) – part will be changes to your practice and part will be confirmation that what you are doing is fine. As a *reflective practitioner* this will become your normal routine of quality assurance and enhancement as you continuously *reflect on practice*. This process could, of course, occur as you are giving the class or holding a meeting, and then you are *reflecting in action* and you change or confirm things as you go along. Bradbury et al. (2012) and Barnard and Ryan (2017) take these ideas much further, and Davis and Fitzpatrick (2019) is a great compendium of ideas and information.

6. *Talking and listening to others*: we will talk further about mentors below, but also think about sharing ideas and concerns with others, both in your own discipline and beyond. There are also several online collections of teachers talking about their practice – see *Further resources*.

Interpreting feedback

You said we did is an oft-used banner line for evaluation processes these days, suggesting that we always respond to feedback. It is always a good idea to tell the students what you have done, or why you have not done what was suggested, in some way: the next handbook for the course is an ideal place, or a special page in the VLE. In addition, it is always worth following up on changes to see that things are improved as a result of the revisions that were made. Maybe a question in the interim evaluation when the course next runs, or setting up a small focus group; it is best not to assume that action always results in improvement.

ONGOING DEVELOPMENT

Dealing with feedback 1

Some of the feedback you receive from students and/or peers and your resultant action plan will be fairly straightforward:

- Availability of library resources – a conversation with the faculty librarian or school library representative will clarify options
- Clarity about assessment methods – a briefing note or frequently-asked-questions (FAQ) page in the VLE and/or a conversation in one of the lectures at the appropriate time
- Release dates for online materials (lecture notes and PowerPoint slides, for example) – checking the institutional/school guidance and norms and responding accordingly.

As we noted above, it is difficult sometimes, as an early-career member of staff, to benchmark feedback and discussions with a peer – mentor or critical friend can be very helpful here. We will come back to mentors later.

Dealing with feedback 2: continuing professional development

Some of the feedback you receive, and the action plan you decide, may require you to do more than the straightforward responses suggested above; you may need to rethink/develop your practice. Alternatively you may decide to develop an aspect of your practice, say producing high-quality online materials using the desktop lecture-capture software that is available in your institution so that you can *flip* classes. In both cases you will need to do some reading, talk to others, go on a course, etc. This is labelled *continuing professional development*, and the term is used to "describe the learning activities professionals engage in to develop and enhance their abilities. It enables learning to become conscious and proactive, rather than passive and reactive" (CPD, 2020; cpduk.co.uk). We think of CPD as a cycle that involves several iterative and structured steps:

a. *Recognition of need*: you decide that you want or need to develop an aspect of practice as a result of: feedback (perhaps from students or a peer), a need due to planned innovation (implement flipped classes), the stage of your career (taking on a leadership role) or reflection (recognising a gap in your skills/professional abilities).
b. *Planned development*: you take a course, read the literature, talk to an expert in the field; whatever it takes ...

166

c. *Impact on practice*: as a result you change your practice or add skills/abilities – you are now able to . . .
d. *Impact on others*: the point was to change/develop your practice, and as a result others will be impacted. So this needs to be monitored by gaining further feedback or checking with peers, etc.
e. *Review*: you need to think the cycle through to see if the plan has worked; you reflect and take new evidence/feedback. This may result in moving on to the next challenge or going back to steps a. and b. above and so moving through the cycle again. As we noted earlier, it is always best not to assume that action results in improvement.

As an early-career academic it is likely that you will be required to go through formal processes such as review by your head of school/department or the principal investigator in your research group or your PhD supervisor, and/or institutional probationary requirements as laid out by Human Resources in your university. This will ensure that you gain feedback, review the meaning of that feedback and create an action plan; but you should be taking control of this ("conscious and proactive, rather than passive and reactive"; ibid.). It is your career, and you need to take responsibility for your development and future; never assume that others will be concerned for your development. As an early-career member of staff it is likely that you will be assigned a mentor, so let us consider that role and what it can mean to you.

Mentors

A mentor may:

- Share information about his/her career path – be a role model
- Discuss and benchmark feedback from students and peers
- Give guidance on options; help with your action plan
- Motivate
- Provide emotional support
- Help explore career paths and options
- Set goals
- Introduce you to contacts and networks
- Identify resources and sources for development/learning.

A mentor should not direct; rather he or she should help you to resolve issues and decide plans. Ideally, in a mentoring relationship you should feel valued and, according to Starr (2014) and Zachary and Fischler (2009), you both:

- Develop mutual trust and respect
- Maintain confidentiality
- Listen both to what is being said and how it is being said.

Many colleagues see mentoring as just a part of early-career development, and move from being mentored to maybe mentoring. Highly successful colleagues invariably continue to invest in mutual mentoring relationships throughout their careers: win-win for both. Thinking about how you would go about selecting a good mentor, Tjan (2018) describes the five types of mentors you need in your life:

- Master of craft
- Champion of your cause
- Co-pilot
- Anchor
- Reverse mentor.

We have included some more details and links in the *Further resources* at the end of this chapter.

In this section we have asked you to think about:

- How you interpret feedback from all sources
- Having some way of collating and combining feedback
- Possible ways to develop your practice
- How to plan your CPD
- Mentoring as an essential ingredient.

Now, we move on to the final theme of the chapter, the important issue of gaining recognition for your high quality.

DOES QUALITY GET RECOGNISED?

Recognition

UKPSF

You will have noticed that each chapter in this text has a link, next to the chapter title, to the UKPSF. This framework, now often just called the PSF as it becomes used more internationally as well as in the UK, was devised to provide HE with a common benchmark for quality in teaching and

ONGOING DEVELOPMENT

supporting student learning. At the time of writing, the last review of the framework took place in 2011, and so that is the year of the version currently in use. However, it is likely that it will be reviewed again and some of these details may change.

The framework has four descriptors or categories of fellowship:

- Descriptor 1 (D1) = Associate Fellow (AFHEA)
- Descriptor 2 (D2) = Fellow (FHEA)
- Descriptor 3 (D3) = Senior Fellow (SFHEA)
- Descriptor 4 (D4) = Principal Fellow (PFHEA).

The awarding of a category includes permission to use the post-nominals which are shown in the brackets above. You may be wondering where the *HEA* part came from; the Higher Education Academy was the predecessor of Advance HE, and rather than create confusion by changing the post-nominals they have been carried forward.

The framework is used to accredit professional-development courses in learning and teaching (as mentioned above), usually at either D1 or D2, and provides a common standard for academics to gain recognition at different categories of fellowship, depending on their role and experience, both by direct application to Advance HE or through accredited, institutional schemes.

The framework is managed by Advance HE, which stated:

> the PSF identifies components of successful teaching and learning. These are expressed in the Dimensions of Professional Practice. The PSF clearly outlines the Dimensions of Professional Practice with HE teaching and learning support as:
>
> - Areas of activity undertaken by teachers and those who support learning (A1 to A5)
> - Core knowledge needed to carry out those activities at the appropriate level (K1 to K6)
> - Professional values that individuals performing these activities should exemplify (V1 to V4).

We have included more information in the *Further resources* section below. You should be thinking about recognition at either AFHEA or FHEA, depending on your role, during the early years of your academic career. As noted above, Fellow has become the standard expectation of a lecturing post carrying research and teaching responsibilities; the PhD is your research credential and Descriptor 2 (FHEA) or Postgraduate Certificate your teaching recognition. See *Further resources* for a link to the Fellowship Category Tool which is provided by Advance HE to allow you to work out which category of fellowship best suits your current practice.

To conclude, the authors of this book, Nuala (SFHEA) and Chris (PFHEA), would both promote the scheme and suggest that you give careful thought to gaining recognition in this way.

SEDA PDF

SEDA (www.seda.ac.uk) also offers a professional-development framework (SEDA PDF: www.seda.ac.uk/what-is-seda-pdf) which "provides recognition for higher education institutions and organisations, accreditation for their professional development programmes and recognition for the individuals who complete those programmes". SEDA offers accreditation, courses, recognition, resources and conferences. Potter and Turner (2018) elaborate on this topic and discuss a range of ways to gain recognition as a good teacher.

Awards for teaching excellence

We include this section to show that recognition, by awards, of high-quality teaching and supporting learning is now standard across the sector. Perhaps you are not in a position to apply at the moment, but you might like to check who has gained these awards where you are when considering possible mentors or sources of good practice. Also, as part of this chapter we are recommending that you have a career plan; some notion of where you want to be in 10 years' time and how you plan to achieve those goals. Is a teaching-excellence award part of that plan?

Institutional awards

There are a number of different institutional award schemes across the sector. Some are run by the HEIs and others by the students' unions. Some are offered at faculty and school/department level. Some are self-nominated whilst others are peer- or student-nominated. There are a range of categories: personal tutor of the year; leadership in learning and teaching, employability, inspiring teaching, assessment and feedback, best non-teaching support staff, curriculum design, use of contemporary research, classroom teaching excellence, technology-enhanced learning, inclusivity. In *Further resources* we have included some examples that are indicative of the type of schemes but, obviously, we suggest that you find out what happens in your institution.

National awards

To complete the picture, national and subject-based awards are available. We include a few indicative examples here, and links are given in *Further resources*.
Disciplinary:

- Law Teacher of the Year
- Biochemical Society Teaching Excellence Award
- Association for Learning Technology, Learning Technologist of the Year Awards.

National:

- Institutional: Global Teaching Excellence Award (GTEA)
- Team: Collaborative Award for Teaching Excellence (CATE)
- National Teaching Fellowship Scheme (NTFS).

TO SUMMARISE

We started out by asking three questions

- How do you know that what you do is good enough (quality assurance)?
- How can you get better (quality enhancement)?
- Does quality get recognised?

We trust that we have given you sufficient answers to get you thinking about how you will:

- Ensure that the student experience that you offer is of the highest quality
- Collect and collate the data to evidence that high quality
- Gain recognition for your achievements.

Finally we recommend that you have

- Clear career goals with a time frame
- A plan to get from where you are to where you want to be in those timed stages
- Thoughts about the necessary CPD and recognition en route.

ONGOING DEVELOPMENT

 FURTHER RESOURCES

Academies or centres of teaching excellence

Examples:
Keele University: Keele Institute for Innovation and Teaching Excellence (KIITE) www.keele.ac.uk/kiite/

University of Derby: Centre for Excellence in Learning and Teaching (CELT) www.derby.ac.uk/services/centre-for-excellence-learning-teaching/

University of Leeds: Leeds Institute for Teaching Excellence (LITE) teachingexcellence.leeds.ac.uk

University of Warwick: WIHEA warwick.ac.uk/fac/cross_fac/academy/

Advance HE

www.advance-he.ac.uk

Postgraduate Taught Experience Survey (PTES)

www.advance-he.ac.uk/reports-publications-and-resources/postgraduate-taught-experience-survey-ptes

Postgraduate Research Experience Survey (PRES)

www.advance-he.ac.uk/reports-publications-and-resources/postgraduate-research-experience-survey-pres

Student voice

www.heacademy.ac.uk/knowledge-hub/student-voice

UKPSF

Based on Advance HE information (www.advance-he.ac.uk/guidance/teaching-and-learning/ukpsf), individual benefits include:

- A way to identify the skills you need to develop and enhance your practice and progress your career
- A globally valued badge of professional recognition allowing you to join a global academy of Fellows

- A means to reflect on your teaching and support of student learning in order to continually develop your educational practice.

Institutional benefits – as a globally-recognised framework for benchmarking success within HE teaching and learning support, the PSF is used by institutions to:

- Enhance the quality and prominence of teaching and learning activities
- Inform the professional-development programmes for staff
- Provide an environment in which staff are encouraged and supported to develop their practice
- Provide an externally benchmarked and accredited mechanism of peer review to demonstrate quality

A copy of the Framework: www.advance-he.ac.uk/knowledge-hub/uk-professional-standards-framework-ukpsf

Awards

Individual: NTFS
www.advance-he.ac.uk/awards/teaching-excellence-awards/national-teaching-fellowship

Institutional: Global Teaching Excellence Award (GTEA)
www.advance-he.ac.uk/awards/teaching-excellence-awards/global-teaching-excellence-awards

Team: The Collaborative Award for Teaching Excellence (CATE)
www.advance-he.ac.uk/awards/teaching-excellence-awards/collaborative-award-for-teaching-excellence

Fellowship Category Tool

Designed to assist you in selecting the category of Fellowship that is the closest match to your current practice
www.advance-he.ac.uk/form/fellowship-decision-tool

International Student Barometer

Run by i-graduate (www.i-graduate.org). Details of the survey and providers: https://www.i-graduate.org/international-student-barometer

Many universities have pages dedicated to the survey and its outcomes.

ONGOING DEVELOPMENT

Mentoring

These resources are aimed at researchers, but good practice in mentoring researchers is good practice . . .

BBSRC

There is a document – Academic Career Mentoring and Best Practice for Formal Mentoring Programmes – available on this page to download that gives good advice.
bbsrc.ukri.org/skills/developing-careers/academic-mentoring/

University of Sheffield

The pages describe a mentoring course (Think Ahead mentoring) but contain some good advice (for free) and some case studies.
www.sheffield.ac.uk/rs/ecr/mentoring

Mid-course evaluation

Seattle University (Seattle U) Center for Faculty Development

Scroll down to Feedback from Students (and notice the other useful stuff as you go . . .) and see a number of ways to gain feedback – and they give you pro formas too.
www.seattleu.edu//faculty-development/resources/

One-minute paper

On Course – a US source of ideas and resources for college courses
oncourseworkshop.com

For the one-minute paper oncourseworkshop.com/self-awareness/one-minute-paper/

MOOC

UNSW Sydney has a long-established Learning to Teach Online MOOC that has already had tens of thousands of international enrolees.
teaching.unsw.edu.au/learning-teach-online-mooc/

Coursera MOOC
www.coursera.org/learn/teach-online

National Student Survey

www.thestudentsurvey.com

Nearly half a million students are asked about their time in HE, at the end of their course, each year. The survey is commissioned by the Office for Students (OfS). Currently it asks 27 core questions related to eight aspects of the student experience, and institutions may add optional ones from six banks of questions, and two questions specific to the institution. The core questions are available at: www.thestudentsurvey.com/content/NSS2020_Core_Questionnaire.pdf

The outcomes of the survey are published on the Discover Uni website: discoveruni.gov.uk

National Survey of Student Engagement (NSSE)

nsse.indiana.edu

For more details and what the survey is about see nsse.indiana.edu/nsse/about-nsse/index.html

National Union of Students

www.nus.org.uk

See also NUS Connect (www.nusconnect.org.uk). In particular:

- The NUS resource hub at studentopportunities.nus.org.uk
- The Learner Voice Framework at www.nusconnect.org.uk/articles/the-learner-voice-framework-has-launched

For more on the student voice from Advance HE, see above.

Peer observation

The University of Nottingham's TLOC

TLOC is committed to supporting and developing excellence in teaching practice and the on-going professional development of all University of Nottingham staff through a collegiate approach. To meet this aim, it emphasises four underpinning themes: dialogue, support, enhance and dissemination.
www.nottingham.ac.uk/professionaldevelopment/learningandteaching/tloc/index.aspx

Peer review

Penn State, US

Faculty Peer Review of Online Teaching: useful guidance and (downloadable) forms
facdev.e-education.psu.edu/evaluate-revise/peerreviewonline

University of Plymouth, UK

Details of its peer review scheme, again with useful guidance and (downloadable) forms
www.plymouth.ac.uk/about-us/teaching-and-learning/guidance-and-resources/peer-review-scheme

Portfolios

Building on Paulson et al. (1991), who provide a useful definition to start thinking about the value of portfolios as a means to assess student achievement, we have translated this for professional development:

> A portfolio is a purposeful collection of work and evidence that substantiates effort, progress and achievement in one or more areas of academic practice. Individuals are responsible for: selecting content; the criteria for selection; the criteria for judging merit. The portfolio must be underpinned by critical self-reflection.

If you want more about portfolios both for assessment and for self-development, we suggest:

1. Hamp-Lyons, L., and Condon, W. 2000. *Assessing the Portfolio: Principles for Practice, Theory and Research.* Cresskill, NJ: Hampton Press.
2. Klenowski, V. 2002. *Developing Portfolios for Learning and Assessment: Processes and Principles.* Abingdon: Routledge-Falmer.
3. Madden, T. 2007. Supporting Student e-Portfolios. *New Directions in the Teaching of Physical Sciences.* The purpose of this guide is to provide a basic introduction to e-portfolios: what they are how they are being used potential benefits and challenges technical implications and how they might be introduced.
s3.eu-west-2.amazonaws.com/assets.creode.advancehe-document-manager/documents/hea/private/eportfolios_jisc_1568036898.pdf
4. Strivens, J., 2006. *Efficient Assessment of Portfolios.* Centre for Recording Achievement. An account of ways in which portfolios are used efficiently, it describes portfolio practice in five professional courses with large student cohorts, identifies efficient practices, discusses trade-offs between educational effectiveness and efficiency, and provides advice on the design of affordable portfolio assessment. www.advance-he.ac.uk/knowledge-hub/efficient-assessment-portfolios

ONGOING DEVELOPMENT

Talking about teaching

Teachers (experienced, early-career and PhD) talking about teaching:
vimeo.com/channels/1067472
vimeo.com/channels/667967

Further teaching award schemes

Institutional
University of Oxford Social Sciences Division
www.socsci.ox.ac.uk/article/teaching-awards-2018-19

University of Warwick: Warwick Awards for Teaching Excellence
warwick.ac.uk/services/od/academic-development/wate/

University of Westminster: Westminster Learning and Teaching Excellence Awards
cti.westminster.ac.uk/westminster-teaching-excellence-awards/

University of York: The Excellence Awards
yusu.org/excellence

National/disciplinary
Association for Learning Technology (ALT): Learning Technologist of the Year Awards
www.alt.ac.uk

Biochemical Society: Teaching Excellence Awardbiochemistry.org/grants-and-awards/awards/teaching-excellence-award/Oxford University Press: Law Teacher of the Year Awardglobal.oup.com/ukhe/lawresources/lawteacher

Tomorrow's Professor

A great source of ideas with postings twice weekly. Rick Reis, who edits this newsletter, notes that the:

> eNewsletter seeks to foster a diverse, world-wide teaching and learning ecology among its over 65,000 subscribers at over 1,000 institutions and organizations in over 100 countries around the world. To date (2020) there have been over 1600 postings under the following categories:
>
> - Tomorrow's Academy
> - Tomorrow's Graduate Students and Postdocs

ONGOING DEVELOPMENT

- Tomorrow's Academic Careers
- Tomorrow's Teaching and Learning
- Tomorrow's Research.

To subscribe, go to: mailman.stanford.edu/mailman/listinfo/tomorrowsprofessor. The archive of posts – easily searched – is at stanford.edu

Chapter 9

Key terms, glossaries and abbreviations

KEY FINDINGS FROM OUR SURVEY

Among the main challenges our respondents faced were:

> I have found myself in small group meetings with my PGCAP [Postgraduate Certificate in Academic Practice] tutor, where I was the only foreigner: I could not understand a word, tons of abbreviations were thrown at us, everybody was fine with them, of course but I was lost. It was as though people considered that my good English speaking skills were enough to grasp the rest.
>
> French lecturer teaching in the UK

> [B]e prepared to deal with an excess of acronyms.
>
> American lecturer teaching in the UK

KEY TERMS

These are the key terms that we have highlighted (in bold and italics) in the text.

Academic misconduct

Has been defined as "any inappropriate activity or behaviour where a student has attempted to gain, or help another student to gain, an unpermitted academic advantage in a summative assessment" (University of Nottingham, 2020).

KEY TERMS, GLOSSARIES AND ABBREVIATIONS

Access and participation plan

A plan that all higher education institutions in England are required to produce to show how they will improve equality of opportunity.

Accommodation

A process whereby the learner has to adapt existing cognitive structures (see also *schema*) to fit new information.

Advance HE

An organisation that aims to enhance the professional practice of higher education and improve outcomes for students, staff and society.

Aims

These are broad, general statements of educational intent and should inform students of the overall purpose of a **programme**, course, **module** or session. Some of the aims will be discipline-specific whilst others can be seen as general, graduate attributes and employability skills. (See also *learning outcomes*.)

Alternative providers

Privately funded higher education providers that do not receive public funding and are not further education colleges.

Approaches to learning

Research that shows that the approach a student takes to learning depends on what it is they are being asked to learn. The two main approaches are a *deep approach* and a *surface approach*.

Assessment

Process of making a judgement on some aspect of a student's work and therefore their learning. (See also **norm-referenced assessment** and **criterion-referenced assessment**.)

Assessment criteria

Identify what aspects of the *assessment task* will be taken into account when the assessor marks the work.

Assessment task

A general term that covers any assessment a student is asked to do; e.g. coursework, exam, test. (See also *diagnostic assessment, formative assessment* and *summative assessment.*)

Assimilation

A process whereby the learner tries to fit new information into existing cognitive structures (see also *schema*).

Asynchronous

At its most simple this means *not at the same time*. Typically applied to *online learning* and/or *blended learning*, it means that all the participants (tutor(s) and learners) do not need to be present online at the same, or a particular, time. They can read and leave posts/messages that others will read/respond to later. Imagine it as a conversation (threads) that takes place over time with maybe hours or days between contributions. Given that some online courses are available worldwide this allows for time zones. (See also *synchronous.*)

Attainment gaps

Gaps between the achievements of some students compared to others.

Blended learning

Enhancing the face-to-face learning opportunities for students by including online material, resources and opportunities for interaction; some may say the best of both worlds.

Compulsory schooling

In the UK all children are required to attend school from the ages of (about) 5 to 16; we say *about* as there are particular rules that apply at both ages. For starting age see www.education-ni.gov.uk/articles/compul

sory-education, and for ending age see www.gov.uk/know-when-you-can-leave-school. (See also *post-compulsory education*.)

Constructive alignment

A term introduced by John Biggs which brings together a constructivist view of learning and the importance of aligning the learning outcomes, teaching and learning activities and assessment.

Constructivism

A theory of learning that claims that leaners construct their own understanding (meaning) of what they are learning based on their previous knowledge and experience.

Course

A dictionary definition is "a set of classes or a plan of study on a particular subject, usually leading to an exam or qualification" (https://dictionary.cambridge.org). Confusingly we also refer to a degree course, so you will find this term used in many ways. (See also *module, unit* and *programme*.)

Coursework

Assessment task done by a student in their own time (not under controlled conditions) during their course. Also referred to as assignments.

Credits/credit ratings

In order to try to achieve some equivalence across degrees in terms of workload we use a tariff – credit – system which gives credit ratings to *units/modules* of study, sets a total credit requirement for a particular qualification (e.g. 360 for a first degree in England) and equates a credit with nominal student workload; one credit = 10 hours of student work. However, not all higher education institutions use a credit system – some use UK credit and others the European credit system (ECTS).

Criterion-referenced assessment

Judgement is made against a set of pre-determined criteria such as *learning outcomes*, percentage grades, qualitative criteria, *marking* rubrics, etc.

KEY TERMS, GLOSSARIES AND ABBREVIATIONS

Curriculum

Some use the term just to mean the taught course that a student is enrolled on. We see the need for a wider definition that includes the:

- Degree (or qualification) subject(s) = taught curriculum
- Learning that complements the chosen degree subject(s) = co-curricular
- Encompasses learning beyond the course timetable = extra-curricular
- Implicit academic, social, and cultural values conveyed during the course = hidden curriculum.

Dearing Report

A 1997 report on a government review of higher education in the UK that made 93 recommendations about the expansion, funding and maintenance of standards.

Deep approach

An approach to learning where the intention of the learner is to try and understand the meaning (see also *surface approach*).

Diagnostic assessment

Used prior to or at the start of a course or period of learning to ascertain what students already know about the topic.

Equality, diversity and inclusion

Equality (or equity) is about treating everyone fairly, diversity about recognising that difference is positive, and inclusivity about including people who might otherwise be excluded.

Examination

Assessment task completed under controlled conditions; i.e. at a set time and venue.

KEY TERMS, GLOSSARIES AND ABBREVIATIONS

External examiner

An academic from another institution whose role is to provide impartial advice on the academic standards and quality of assessment.

Feedback

The process of giving a student some information about their work with a view to helping them improve.

Flip the class/flipped classroom

Typically the content is introduced in the classroom (lecture theatre) and then the students practise and use the ideas away from the classroom (directed learning/homework). This means that the teacher presents the content but is not available when the learner is trying to come to terms with the ideas and concepts, which some see as the harder part of learning. Modern technology – with the ease of producing videos – allows teachers to record their delivery of the content, which the student can then watch before coming to class. This means that the student arrives with background content and ideas and questions which the teacher can then build on/respond to.

Formative assessment

Aimed at giving students' feedback about their learning.

Frameworks for higher education qualifications

The Qualification Frameworks set out the different levels of higher education qualifications and the requirements for each of these. There is one framework for England, Wales and Northern Ireland and a separate one for Scotland.

(QAA, 2020)

Grading

Grouping students' work into bands of achievement and awarding a symbol (e.g. A, B or C; or 1st, 2:1 or 2:2) to represent a larger-scale judgement such as overall performance on a course.

KEY TERMS, GLOSSARIES AND ABBREVIATIONS

Ground rules

When we are driving on the roads we have to follow a set of rules (in the UK we call this the Highway Code), otherwise there is chaos. In the same way, if we do not have some rules for tutorials and seminars then life would be rather chaotic; all talking at the same time, turning up when one felt like it, not preparing by reading the papers/article, etc. The concept of agreeing ground rules means that as a group – tutor and learners – we all agree to a set way of working.

Higher education institutions (HEIs)

A collective term used to include all institutions that provide higher education, including universities, colleges and institutes of technology. Often used interchangeably with *universities*.

Icebreakers

When we meet a (small) group of *new* people – say the first tutorial or seminar class – it takes time for people to get to know one another and start feeling secure to talk, share and put their ideas and thinking out for others to hear and discuss/critique. Icebreakers can get people involved in a (usually fun) activity that lubricates talking and interaction. For example: "Form into pairs and then introduce your partner to the rest of the group" requires you to talk to your partner and find something out about them.

Ask your students to think of two to three hashtags that describe them. Allow them to write their hashtags on the board/flipchart and explain them to the rest of the class. You, the tutor, need to take part too – maybe you start . . .

Inclusive teaching

A term used to describe teaching in a way that enables all students to participate and fulfil their potential by removing any barriers that prevent them from learning.

Induction

Literally means "lead in", so it makes sense to lead students into university life.

KEY TERMS, GLOSSARIES AND ABBREVIATIONS

Key stages

Compulsory schooling in England and Wales has been split into four stages in which children are grouped depending upon their age. Table 2.1 in Chapter 2 shows the links between the stages, the pupils' ages and the school year. Between each stage there are expectations of *progression* in certain subjects – what children should know and be able to do – and at the end of key stages 1, 2 and 4 the children take standardised tests or examinations that give an indication of achievement.

Knowledge exchange

Refers to the exchange of knowledge and expertise between researchers and users of that research in society. Used to describe the third element of higher education; teaching and research are the other two.

Learning outcomes

As defined by Butcher et al. (2020), these are

> more focused and indicate what a student is expected to be able to do at various points during and/or at the end of a course of study. Typically, learning outcomes specify the minimum requirement at the point of assessment for the award of credit: threshold requirements. They may refer to subject specific concepts and skills, or more general (transferable/generic) attributes and abilities.

Lecture capture

The process of recording lectures as videos and making them available for students. If made available after the live class, this means that learners can review aspects that they did not understand or need more time to think about. Students whose first language is not the one recorded on the video can also find this very helpful as it allows them to watch and listen at their own pace, conveniently and for as many times as it takes. Making them available before the timetabled class allows you to *flip the class*.

Level descriptors

The QAA (2014) says: "A statement of the generic characteristics of outcomes of learning at a specific level of a qualifications framework, used as a reference point." These statements allow us to think about progression as for each level (4 to 6) for an undergraduate degree we have set expectations and so can match our *aims* and *learning outcomes* to suit.

Major/minor changes (to courses)

A course, *module* or *unit* has to be quality-assured and approved by the appropriate committee(s) of a higher education institution before it can be offered to students. If you wish to make a change to it you must check whether the change counts as *major* (this requires that it goes back through, at least, some of the quality-assurance mechanism) or *minor* (you can make the change in time for the next iteration of the course).

Marking

Awarding a number (usually) or symbol to represent the student's achievement, normally in an individual piece of work rather than the overall course. Also referred to as *scoring*.

Moderation

A checking process to make sure *assessment criteria* have been applied appropriately and *marking* is fair and consistent.

Modularisation

Courses are divided into chunks (*modules* or *units*) and these are taught within and assessed at the end of semesters. Students have more choice as to which modules they take, although it is usual for there to be core or required modules to gain a certain degree qualification.

Module

A module is a self-contained, sub-unit of a degree that usually runs across one, or at the most two, semester(s). It tends to focus on one subject or aspect of a discipline and usually is assessed independently. Modules usually carry a *credit rating* and are grouped together to create qualifications. Students will often be studying several modules concurrently.

KEY TERMS, GLOSSARIES AND ABBREVIATIONS

National Curriculum

The National Curriculum is a set of subjects and standards used by primary and secondary schools in order that children study the same things. It covers what subjects are taught and the standards (attainment targets) children should reach in each subject at different ages.

National Student Survey (NSS)

Annual census of final-year undergraduate students at all publicly funded higher education institutions in the UK.

Norm-referenced assessment

Judgement of a student's work is made in comparison to other students in the group; i.e. ranked.

Online learning

This is education that is offered over the internet; also called e-learning. It is a form of distance learning where tutors create virtual classrooms — where the online teaching takes place — using video, audio and written materials. Invariably these courses are enabled by a course management system (CMS) or *virtual learning environment* (VLE). The value of CMS/VLE software is that it offers ways to communicate (announcements, message and discussion boards) and run tests and quizzes as well as store the teaching materials, and they are secure (password-protected).

Personal tutor

Normally an academic member of staff who supports some students through their course by providing academic, pastoral and/or developmental support. (See also *senior tutors*.)

Personal tutoring system

Usually involves each student being allocated a *personal tutor* to support them throughout their period of study.

KEY TERMS, GLOSSARIES AND ABBREVIATIONS

Polytechnics

A type of higher education institution which tended to focus more on technical and vocational degree courses, most of which were formed from local colleges and technical institutions in England, Wales and Northern Ireland in the 1960s following a review of higher education (Robbins, 1963). They did not have degree-awarding status; instead this was done by a central council (UK Council for National Academic Awards). The polytechnics all became universities in 1992, when they were granted degree-awarding status.

Post-compulsory education

Education that follows compulsory education; after 18 in England and after 16 in the rest of the UK, at present. (See also *compulsory schooling*.)

Professional body

A Professional Body is an organisation with individual members practicing a profession or occupation in which the organisation maintains an oversight of the knowledge, skills, conduct and practice of that profession or occupation.

(Science Council; https://sciencecouncil.org)

(See also *Professional, statutory and regulatory bodies*.)

Professional, statutory and regulatory bodies (PSRBs)

A very diverse group of professional and employer bodies, regulators and those with statutory authority over a profession or group of professionals. PSRBs engage with higher education as regulators. They provide membership services and promote the interests of people working in professions; accredit or endorse courses that meet professional standards, provide a route through to the professions or are recognised by employers.

Examples of PSRBs are the General Medical Council, the Architects Registration Board, the British Association of Art Therapists, and the Institute of Physics.

(HESA; www.hesa.ac.uk)

KEY TERMS, GLOSSARIES AND ABBREVIATIONS

Professional support services

Central university services whose role is to support all aspects of university life, including supporting students and staff in their day-to-day living, and being more specifically focused on helping students be successful in their academic studies.

Programme

A programme, or, more completely, *programme of study*, is typically a whole degree. (See also *module* and *unit*.)

Programme specification

An approved, definitive record of each *programme* or qualification specifying what the *learning outcomes* are and how they will be achieved.

Progression

Learning often follows an expected track or path; more complex skills are built on foundational skills. For example, children learn to crawl, then stand, then take some steps before taking off and running. Progression is about building from basic to complex, be that in skills, knowledge, understanding, etc.

Quality assurance

Approving to a minimum standard.

Quality Code

> The Quality Code is a key reference point for UK higher education, protecting the public and student interest, and championing UK higher education's world-leading reputation for quality. It enables providers to understand what is expected of them and what to expect from each other.
>
> (QAA, 2020)

Quality enhancement

Making courses better.

Reflective practice

The ability to review one's actions and behaviours (successes and failures) in order to learn from experience and so improve. Learning from experience rather than repeating the same errors or mistakes.

Reflective practitioner

Someone who continuously engages in *reflective practice*. One might *reflect in action* (reviewing and changing as one goes) or *on practice* (thinking and reviewing after the event). In both cases the aim is to learn and improve.

Robbins Report

A 1963 report on a government review of higher education in the UK that introduced the notion that university places should be available to all those who had the ability (the Robbins principle). As a result, free tuition and maintenance grants were introduced for students.

Schema

A term used to describe the cognitive structures or framework for one's knowledge.

Semesters

Used when an academic year is divided into two halves. The first semester typically starts around September/October and runs until January, and the second starts around February and ends in June. (See also *terms*.)

Senior tutors

Co-ordinate and support a network of *personal tutors* within a school or institution

Student-centred approach

Where the focus is on the students and how they learn as opposed to on the teacher and what they do (see also *teacher-centred approach*).

KEY TERMS, GLOSSARIES AND ABBREVIATIONS

Students' Union

An organisation run by students for students, providing support for students at that institution.

Subject benchmark statements

Describe the nature of study and the academic standards expected of graduates in specific subject areas. They show what graduates might reasonably be expected to know, do and understand at the end of their studies.

(QAA, 2020)

Summative assessment

Used to measure a student's learning at the end of a block of learning or *module*.

Surface approach

An approach to learning where the intention of the learner is to memorise the information presented to them so they can reproduce it later (see also *deep approach*).

Synchronous

Happening at the same time; the opposite of *asynchronous*. A telephone conversation is synchronous communication.

Synoptic assessment

A form of assessment which tests understanding and application of connections between different elements of a subject. If two *modules* or *units* are assessed by one test or set of tests, this would be synoptic assessment of the learning outcomes of the two modules. The final-year project or dissertation would be another good example, as this draws on a student's knowledge, skills and approaches developed across the whole degree course.

Teacher-centred approach

Where the focus is on the teacher and what they do rather than on the students and how they learn (see also *student-centred approach*).

Teaching Excellence and Student Outcomes Framework

A national assessment of excellence in teaching at universities and colleges in which institutions are awarded a bronze, silver or gold award.

Terms

The traditional way of dividing the academic year into three parts, Term 1 typically being from September/October until before Christmas (25 December), Term 2 from January to before Easter (sometime around March/April) and Term 3 from Easter until June. (See also *semesters*.)

Test

Assessment task completed in-class or online in semi-controlled conditions and often of a shorter duration than exams.

360-degree feedback

A process by which someone receives anonymous feedback from the people who work with them. This could include the person who manages them, those that they manage and their peers who work alongside them; up, down and sideways feedback.

Transnational education (TNE)

This is education delivered in a different country from the one where the provider is based. In higher education terms this means the delivery of degrees in a transnational setting.

Triangulation

When collecting information about your teaching (evaluation), the idea of triangulation is that you take more than one source of evidence; typically this could be your students, a peer and your own view. In this way you have several sets of views and so can reduce bias when you interpret and act on the information.

KEY TERMS, GLOSSARIES AND ABBREVIATIONS

UK Professional Standards Framework (UKPSF)

A nationally recognised framework for benchmarking success within teaching and learning support.

Unit

Some universities do not use *module* for the sub-units or parts of a degree but instead use *unit*. (See also **module** and **programme**.)

Universities and Colleges Admission Service (UCAS)

The central application service for the vast majority of applications for full-time undergraduate courses in the UK (home and international students) and for some postgraduate applications.

UCAS tariff

Many qualifications have a UCAS tariff value. The value depends on the demand of the qualification (years of study and level of the qualification – see also **Frameworks for higher education qualifications**) and the grade achieved. Some higher education institutions (HEIs) use UCAS tariffs to set the entry level for courses, but not all qualifications have tariffs and not all HEIs use the tariff system (they prefer to use qualifications and grades).

Virtual learning environment (VLE)

A web-based platform used by education institutions to host digital aspects of courses of study.

Widening participation

A term used to describe attempts to increase the proportion of students in UK HE that come from under-represented groups such as people with disabilities, lower-income families and some ethnic minorities. (*Widening access* is the term used in Scotland.)

GLOSSARIES

If you did not find a meaning in the list of key terms above, these are the most useful glossaries that we could find.

KEY TERMS, GLOSSARIES AND ABBREVIATIONS

Glossary of Education Reform: www.edglossary.org
Claims to be a "comprehensive online resource that describes widely used school-improvement terms, concepts, and strategies for journalists, parents, and community members". It is one of the most comprehensive glossaries that we have found for generic education terminology. It is US-based and that means some of the specific terms are different to standard UK usage, but overall it is well worth having on speed-dial.

Australian Government Tertiary Education Quality and Standards Agency (TEQSA): www.teqsa.gov.au/glossary-terms
A glossary of terms as used in Australasia; if you have any concerns from the Glossary of Education Reform (above) information then this should certainly help.

Wikipedia glossary of educational terms: en.wikipedia.org/wiki/Glossary_of_education_terms
The most comprehensive UK source we found; it covers all aspects of education.

Learn Higher: www.learnhigher.ac.uk
A search for *glossary* brings up:

- Research terms glossary
- Using an academic glossary – the resource includes a glossary of academic terms.

Both are downloadable with Creative Commons licences.

A TO Z OF RESOURCES

London School of Economics and Political Sciences (LSE): info.lse.ac.uk/staff/divisions/Eden-Centre/Resources-from-Eden/A-to-Z-of-resources
Not a glossary as such, just a fabulous collection of resources, arranged from A to Z. This covers a plethora of topics, from teaching methods to assessing to terminology.

University College Dublin (UCD): www.ucd.ie/teaching/resources/resourcesa-z/
Another great resource covering many aspects of learning and teaching in higher education.

ARCHIVED GLOSSARY

The Economics Network (now closed) produced a good glossary of terms particularly related to the discipline – it called it the Acronym Buster. We include it as you may find what you are looking for here if nowhere else.
web.archive.org/web/20061006073902/http://www.economicsnetwork.ac.uk/advice/acronyms.htm

KEY TERMS, GLOSSARIES AND ABBREVIATIONS

EDUCATIONAL ABBREVIATIONS

You might like to use these as your starter; it is well worth creating your own list.

AHE Advance HE
BA Bachelor of Arts (studying a subject in the arts, humanities or social sciences; LLB for Bachelor of Law)
BEng Bachelor of Engineering
BSc Bachelor of Science
BTEC Business and Technology Education Council
BAME Black, Asian and minority ethnic
CPD Continuing professional development
DDA Disability Discrimination Act
DfE Department for Education
DPA Data Protection Act
EBacc English Baccalaureate
ECTS The European Credit Transfer and Accumulation System
ESFA Education, Skills and Funding Agency
FE Further education
FHEQ Framework for Higher Education Qualifications in England, Wales and Northern Ireland
FQHEIS Framework for Qualifications of Higher Education Institutions in Scotland
FOI Freedom of Information
FTE Full-time equivalent
G&T Gifted and talented
GCSE General Certificate of Secondary Education, usually taken at the end of Key Stage 4
GDPR General Data Protection Regulation
H&S Health and safety
HEI Higher education institution
HE Higher education
HR Human resources
ICT Information and communications technology
IiP Investors in People
IT Information technology
KS Key Stage
LA Local authority
MA Master of Arts (studying a subject in the arts, humanities or social sciences; LLM for Master of Law)
MSc Master of Science
MPhil Master of Philosophy (advanced research master's degree)
MRes Master of Research
MFL Modern foreign languages
NC National Curriculum
NEET Not in education, employment or training

196

KEY TERMS, GLOSSARIES AND ABBREVIATIONS

NVQ National Vocational Qualifications
Ofqual Office of Qualifications & Examinations Regulation
OfS Office for Students
OFSTED Office for Standards in Education (pre-tertiary education)
PGCHE Postgraduate Certificate of Higher Education
PT Part-time
QA Quality assurance
QAA Quality Assurance Agency
R&R Recruitment and retention
SATs Standard Assessment Tests
SEN/D Special educational needs or disability
STEM Science, Technology, Engineering and Mathematics
TNE Transnational education
UKPSF UK Professional Standards Framework
VA Value added (of education)
VLE Virtual learning environment

References

Advance HE. 2018a. *Equality + higher education: students statistical report.* York: Author.
Advance HE. 2018b. Flipped learning. [Online] www.heacademy.ac.uk/knowledge-hub/flipped-learning.
Advance HE. 2020. Public sector equality duty. [Online] www.advance-he.ac.uk/guidance/equality-diversity-and-inclusion/equality-legislation/public-sector-equality-duty.
Anderson, L.W. and Krathwohl, D.R. 2001. *A taxonomy for learning, teaching and assessing.* London: Longman.
Ashwin, P., Boud, D., Coate, K., Hallett, F., Keane, E., Krause, K.-L., Leibowitz, B., MacLaren, I., McArthur, J., McCune, V. and Tooher, M. 2015. *Reflective teaching in higher education.* London: Bloomsbury Academic.
Azer, S.A. 2005. Challenges facing PBL tutors: 12 tips for successful group facilitation. *Medical Teacher* 27, 8: 676–681.
Baillie, C., De St Jorre, T.J. and Hazel, E. 2017. *Improving teaching and learning in science and engineering laboratories.* New South Wales: HERDSA.
Barnard, R. and Ryan, J. (eds). 2017. *Reflective practice: voices from the field.* London: Routledge.
Biggs, J. 1999. *Teaching for quality learning at university.* Buckingham: Society for Research in Higher Education/Open University Press.
Biggs, J.B. and Tang, C. 2011. *Teaching for quality learning at university: what the student does.* 4th edn. Maidenhead: Society for Research into Higher Education/Open University Press.
Bligh, D. 1998. *What's the use of lectures?* 5th edn. Bristol: Intellect Books.
Bloom, B.S. (ed). 1956. *Taxonomy of educational objectives: handbook 1 – the cognitive domain.* London: Longman.
Bloxham, S. and Boyd, P. 2007. *Developing effective assessment in higher education: a practical guide.* Maidenhead: Open University Press.
Bolton, P. 2020. *Higher education student numbers.* London: House of Commons Library. [Online]commonslibrary.parliament.uk/research-briefings/cbp–7857/.
Boud, D., Dunn, J. and Hegarty-Hazel, E. 1986. *Teaching in laboratories.* Milton Keynes: SRHE.

REFERENCES

Bradbury, H., Frost, N., Kilminster, S. and Zukas, M. (eds). 2012. *Beyond reflective practice: new approaches to professional lifelong learning.* London: Routledge.

Brown, G. 1991. Explaining. In: Hargie, O. (ed.). *Handbook of communication skills.* London: Croom–Helm.

Brown, S. and Race, P. 2012. Using effective assessment to promote learning. In: Hunt, L. and Chalmers, D. (eds.). *University teaching in focus: a learning-centred approach.* Melbourne: ACER Press.

Butcher, C., Davies, C. and Highton, M. 2020. *Designing learning from module outline to effective teaching.* 2nd edn. Abingdon: Routledge.

Butcher, C. and Timm, H. (eds). 2013. *The learning and teaching e-book.* Out of publication.

Cross-Border Education Research Team. 2017. Branch campuses. [Online] cbert.org/resources-data/branch-campus/.

Davies, C. 2008. Learning and teaching laboratories. Engineering Subject Centre teaching guide. [Online] www.advance-he.ac.uk/knowledge-hub/learning-and-teaching-laboratories-engineering-subject-centre-teaching-guide.

Davis, C.L. and Fitzpatrick, M. (eds). 2019. Reflective practice. *SEDA Special* 42. [Online] www.seda.ac.uk/specials.

Dearing, R. 1997. Higher education in the learning society. [Online] www.educationengland.org.uk/documents/dearing1997/dearing1997.html

Dennick, R. 2014. Theories of learning: constructive experience. In: Matheson, D. (ed.). *An introduction to the study of education.* London: Taylor & Francis.

Dept for Education and Dept for International Trade. 2019. International Education Strategy: global potential, global growth. [Online] www.gov.uk/government/publications/international-education-strategy-global-potential-global-growth.

Donavan, J. 2013. *How to deliver a TED talk: secrets of the world's most inspiring presentations.* New York: McGraw Hill.

Earwaker, J. 1992. *Helping and supporting students: rethinking the issues.* Buckingham: Society for Research into Higher Education/Open University Press.

Edward, N.S. 2003. First impressions last: an innovative approach to induction. *Active Learning in Higher Education* 4: 226–242.

Entwistle, N. 1997. Contrasting perspectives on learning. In: Marton, F., Hounsell, D. and Entwistle, N. (eds.). *The experience of learning.* Edinburgh: Scottish Academic Press.

Equality Act. 2010. [Online] www.legislation.gov.uk/ukpga/2010/15/contents.

Exley, K. 2010. Encouraging active learning in lectures. *All Ireland Journal of Teaching and Learning in HE (AISHE-J)* 2, 1. [Online] ojs.aishe.org/index.php/aishe-j/issue/view/2.

Exley, K. and Dennick, R. 2008. *Giving a lecture: from presenting to teaching.* 2nd edn. Abingdon: RoutledgeFalmer.

Exley, K., Dennick, R. and Fisher, A. 2019. *Small group teaching: tutorials, seminars and workshops.* 2nd edn. Abingdon: Routledge.

Falchikov, N. 2001. *Learning together: peer tutoring in higher education.* Abingdon: RoutledgeFalmer.

Fry, H., Ketteridge, S. and Marshall, S. (eds). 2004. *A handbook for teaching and learning in higher education.* 2nd edn. Abingdon: Routledge.

REFERENCES

Fry, H., Ketteridge, S. and Marshall, S. (eds). 2015. *A handbook for teaching and learning in higher education: enhancing academic practice.* 4th edn. Abingdon: Routledge.

Fullerton, H. 2003. Observation of teaching. In: Fry, H., Ketteridge, S. and Marshall, S. (eds.). *A handbook for teaching and learning in higher education: enhancing academic practice.* 2nd edn. New York: Routledge.

George, J.H. and Doto, F.X. 2001. A simple five-step method for teaching clinical skills. *Family Medicine* 33, 8: 577–578. [Online] www.stfm.org/Portals/49/Documents/FMPDF/FamilyMedicineVol33Issue8George577.pdf.

Gibbs, G. and Simpson, C. 2005. Conditions under which assessment supports students' learning. *Learning and Teaching in Higher Education Quarterly* 1. [Online]. eprints.glos.ac.uk/id/eprint/3609.

Grey, D. and Osborne, C. 2018. Perceptions and principles of personal tutoring. *Journal of Further and Higher Education* 44, 3: 1–15.

Habeshaw, S., Habeshaw, T. and Gibbs, G. 1992. *53 interesting things to do in your seminars and tutorials.* Bristol: Technical and Educational Services.

Haines, C. 2004. *Assessing students' written work: marking essays and reports.* London: RoutledgeFalmer.

Hall, S. and Weale, S. 2019. Universities spending millions on marketing to attract students. *The Guardian.* [Online] www.theguardian.com/education/2019/apr/02/universities-spending-millions-on-marketing-to-attract-students.

Hammersley-Fletcher, L. and Orsmond, P. 2004. Evaluating our peers: is peer observation a meaningful process? *Studies in Higher Education* 29, 4: 489–503.

Hamp-Lyons, L. and Condon, W. 2000. *Assessing the portfolio: principles for practice, theory and research.* Cresskill, NJ: Hampton Press.

HESA. 2020. Higher education student statistics: where students come from and go to study 2018/19. [Online] www.hesa.ac.uk/news/16-01-2020/sb255-higher-education-student-statistics/location.

Hornstein, H.A. and Law, H.F. 2017. Student evaluations of teaching are an inadequate assessment tool for evaluating faculty performance. *Cogent Education* 4, 1. [Online]. doi.org/10.1080/2331186X.2017.1304016.

Hughes, G., Panjwani, M., Priya, T. and Byrom, N. 2018. *Student mental health: the role and experiences of academics.* Leeds: Student Minds.

Hunt, L. and Chalmers, D. 2012. *University teaching in focus: a learning-centred approach.* Melbourne: ACER Press.

Huntley-Moore, S. and Panter, J. 2015. An introduction to module design. *All Ireland Society for Higher Education, Academic (AISHE) Practice Guides.* 3. [Online]. www.aishe.org/wp-content/uploads/2016/01/3-Module-Design.pdf.

Illeris, K. 2017. *How we learn.* London: Routledge.

Irons, A. 2007. *Enhancing learning through formative assessment and feedback.* Abingdon: Routledge.

Jaques, D. 2003. Teaching small groups. *British Medical Journal.* 326. [Online]. www.bmj.com/content/326/7387/492.1.abstract.

Jaques, D. and Salmon, G. 2007. *Learning in groups: a handbook for face-to-face and online environments.* 4th edn. London: Kogan Page.

Klenowski, V. 2002. *Developing portfolios for learning and assessment: processes and principles.* Abingdon: RoutledgeFalmer.

REFERENCES

Kolb, D.A. 1984. *Experiential learning: experience as the source of learning and development.* Upper Saddle River, NJ: Prentice Hall.

Land, R., Meyer, J. and Smith, J. (eds). 2008. *Threshold concepts within the disciplines.* Rotterdam: Sense Publishers.

Lave, J. and Wenger, E. 1991. *Situated learning: legitimate peripheral participation.* New York, NY: Cambridge University Press.

Light, G. and Cox, R. 2001. *Learning and teaching in higher education: the reflective professional.* London: Paul Chapman.

Lightbody, G. and Nicholl, P. 2013. Extending the concept of the one minute paper model. Paper from HEA 2013 STEM Annual Conference. [Online] www.advance-he.ac.uk/knowledge-hub/extending-concept-one-minute-paper-model.

Lochtie, D., McIntosh, E., Stork, A. and Walker, B. 2018. *Effective personal tutoring in higher education.* St Albans: Critical Publishing.

Lublin, J. and Sutherland, K. 2009. *Conducting tutorials.* New South Wales: HERDSA.

Luidia.com. n.d. 58 ways teachers use document cameras. [Online] www.santeesd.net/cms/lib/CA01000468/Centricity/Domain/35/58_Ways_Teachers_Doc_Cam.pdf.

Madden, T. 2007. Supporting student e-portfolios. *New Directions in the Teaching of Physical Sciences* 3. [Online] https://doi.org/10.29311/ndtps.v0i3.408.

Marton, F., Dall'Alba, G. and Beaty, E. 1993. Conceptions of learning. *International Journal of Educational Research* 19: 277–300.

Marton, F. and Säljö, R. 1976. On qualitative differences in learning: i-outcome and process. *British Journal of Educational Psychology* 46: 4–11.

Maslow, A.H. 1954. *Motivation and personality.* New York: Harper & Row. [Online]www.eyco.org/nuovo/wp-content/uploads/2016/09/Motivation-and-Personality-A.H.Maslow.pdf.

May, S.A. and Silva-Fletcher, A. 2015. Scaffolded active learning: nine pedagogical principles for building a modern veterinary curriculum. *JVME* 42: 4.

Mazur, E. 2012. Confessions of a converted lecturer. [Video] www.youtube.com/watch?v=ZpNjem3p0Ak.

Means, B., Bakia, M. and Murphy, R. 2014. *Learning online: what research tells us about whether, when and how.* New York, NY: Routledge.

Merriam, S.B., Caffarella, R.S.B. and Baumgartner, L.M. 2006. *Learning in adulthood: a comprehensive guide.* San Francisco: John Wiley & Sons.

Meyer, J. and Land, R. 2003. Threshold concepts and troublesome knowledge: linkages to ways of thinking and practising within the disciplines. In: Rust, C. (ed.). *Improving student learning: theory and practice ten years on.* Oxford: Oxford Centre for Staff and Learning Development. [Online] www.etl.tla.ed.ac.uk/docs/ETLreport4.pdf.

Meyer, J. and Land, R. 2006. *Overcoming barriers to student understanding: threshold concepts and troublesome knowledge.* Abingdon: Routledge.

Newcastle University. 2018. Guidance on writing learning outcomes. [Online] www.ncl.ac.uk/ltds/assets/documents/res-writinglearningoutcomes.pdf.

Nicol, D.J. and Macfarlane-Dick, D. 2006. Formative assessment and self-regulated learning: a model and seven principles of good feedback practice. *Studies in Higher Education* 31: 199–218.

REFERENCES

NSS. 2019. National Student Survey. Office for Students. [Online] www.officeforstudents.org.uk/advice-and-guidance/student-information-and-data/national-student-survey-nss/.

Office for Students. 2020. The Regulatory Framework for Higher Education in England. [Online] www.officeforstudents.org.uk/advice-and-guidance/regulation/the-regulatory-framework-for-higher-education-in-england/.

Paulson, F.L., Paulson, P.R. and Meyer, C.A. 1991. What makes a portfolio. *Educational Leadership* 48, 5: 60–63.

Perry, W.G. 1970. *Forms of intellectual and ethical development in the college years: a scheme.* New York, NY: Holt, Rinehart and Winston.

Pitt, E. and Winstone, N. 2018. The impact of anonymous marking on students' perceptions of fairness, feedback and relationships with lecturers. *Assessment & Evaluation in Higher Education* 43: 1183–1193.

Pokorny, H. 2016. Assessment for learning. In: Pokorny, H. and Warren, D. (eds.). *Enhancing teaching practice in HE.* London: Sage.

Potter, J. and Turner, R. (eds). 2018. Doing a good job well: being recognised as an experienced, professional teacher in HE. *SEDA Special 41.* [Online] www.seda.ac.uk/specials.

Price, M., Rust, C., O'Donovan, B., Hindley, K. and Bryant, R. 2012. *Assessment literacy: the foundation for improving student learning.* Oxford: Oxford Centre for Staff and Learning Development.

QAA. 2008. Higher education credit framework for England: guidance on academic credit arrangements in higher education in England. August 2008. [Online] www.qaa.ac.uk/quality-code/qualifications-and-credit-frameworks.

QAA. 2014. The frameworks for higher education qualifications of UK degree-awarding bodies. [Online] www.qaa.ac.uk/quality-code/qualifications-and-credit-frameworks.

QAA. 2018. UK quality code for higher education: advice and guidance – assessment. [Online] www.qaa.ac.uk/quality-code/advice-and-guidance/assessment.

QAA. 2020. Subject benchmark statements [Online]. www.qaa.ac.uk/quality-code/subject-benchmark-statements.

QS World University Rankings. 2020. [Online] www.qs.com/rankings/.

Race, P. 2000. *500 tips on group learning.* London: Kogan Page.

Robbins, L. 1963. Higher education: report of the committee appointed by the Prime Minister under the chairmanship of Lord Robbins, 1961–63. [Online] www.educationengland.org.uk/documents/robbins/robbins1963.html.

Ryan, J. 2005. The student experience. In: Carroll, J., Ryan, J. and Ryan, J. (eds.). *Teaching international students.* Abingdon: Routledge.

Sadler, D.R. 2005. Interpretations of criteria-based assessment and grading in higher education. *Assessment & Evaluation in Higher Education* 30: 175–194.

Säljö, R. 1979. *Learning in the learner's perspective 1: some commonplace misconceptions (Report 76).* Gothenburg: University of Gothenburg, Institute of Education.

Salmon, G. 2002. *E-tivities: the key to active online learning.* London: Taylor & Francis.

Salmon, G. 2003. *E-moderating: the key to teaching and learning online.* 2nd edn. London: Taylor & Francis.

REFERENCES

Schön, D.A. 1983. *The reflective practitioner: how professionals think in action*. London: Routledge.

Scottish Funding Council. 2019. Strategic Framework 2019–2022. [Online] www.sfc.ac.uk/web/FILES/StrategicFramework/Scottish_Funding_Council_Strategic_Framework_2019-2022.pdf.

Short, F. and Martin, J. 2011. Presentation vs. performance: effects of lecturing style in higher education on student preference and student learning. *Psychology Teaching Review* 17, 2: 71–82.

Stanford University Teaching Commons. n.d.. Checklist for effective lecturing. [Online] teachingcommons.stanford.edu/resources/teaching-resources/teaching-strategies/checklist-effective-lecturing.

Starr, J. 2014. *The mentoring manual: your step by step guide to being a better mentor*. Harlow: Pearson.

Stead, D.R. 2005. A review of the one-minute paper. *Active Learning in Higher Education* 6, 2: 118–131.

Stein, D.S. and Wanstreet, C.E. 2017. *Jump-start your online classroom: mastering five challenges in five days*. Sterling, VA: Stylus.

Stewart, M. 2012. Understanding learning: theories and critique. In: Hunt, L. and Chalmers, D. (eds.). *University teaching in focus: a learning-centred approach*. Melbourne: ACER Press.

Stork, A. and Walker, B. 2015. *Becoming an outstanding personal tutor: supporting learners through personal tutoring and coaching*. Northwich: Critical Publishing.

Strivens, J. 2006. *Efficient assessment of portfolios*. Wigan: Centre for Recording Achievement.

Swanwick, T. (ed). 2014. *Understanding medical education: evidence, theory and practice*. 2nd edn. Chichester: Wiley-Blackwell.

Thomas, L. 2006. Thomas, L. and Hixenbaugh, P. (eds.) *Personal tutoring in higher education*. London: Institute of Education Press.

Thomas, L. 2012. *Building student engagement and belonging in higher education at a time of change: final report from the What Works? Student Retention & Success programme*. London: Paul Hamlyn Foundation.

Times Higher Education. 2020. THE World University Rankings. [Online] www.timeshighereducation.com/world-university-rankings/2020/world-ranking#!/page/0/length/25/sort_by/rank/sort_order/asc/cols/stats.

Tjan, A. 2018. The 5 types of mentors you need in your life. Ideas.TED.com. [Online] ideas.ted.com/the-5-types-of-mentors-you-need-in-your-life/.

Tryfona, C., Tryfonas, T., Hughes, N. and Levy, J. 2013. Personal tutoring and key skills development in higher education – experiences and challenges. Paper from HEA 2013 STEM Annual Conference. [Online] www.advance-he.ac.uk/knowledge-hub/personal-tutoring-and-key-skills-development-higher-education-experiences-and.

UKPSF. 2011. The UK Professional Standards Framework for teaching and supporting learning in higher education [Online]. www.advance-he.ac.uk/guidance/teaching-and-learning/ukpsf.

REFERENCES

Universities UK International. 2018. The scale of UK higher education transnational education 2016–17: trend analysis of HESA data. [Online] www.universitiesuk.ac.uk/International/Documents/UUKi.

Universities UK International. 2019. The scale of UK HE TNE 2017–18: trend analysis of HESA data. [Online] www.universitiesuk.ac.uk/policy-and-analysis/reports/Documents/2019/the-scale-of-uk-he-tne-2017-18.pdf.

Universities UK. 2019. Higher education in facts and figures. 2019. [Online] www.universitiesuk.ac.uk/facts-and-stats/data-and-analysis/Documents/higher-education-facts-and-figures-2019.pdf.

University of Nottingham. 2020. Academic misconduct policy. [Online] www.nottingham.ac.uk/academicservices/qualitymanual/assessmentandawards/academic-misconduct.aspx.

WHECF. 1996. *Welsh Higher Education Credit Framework handbook*. Higher Education Credit Initiative Wales. Generic level descriptors, p.11.

Wisker, G., Exley, K., Antoniou, M. and Ridley, P. 2008. *Working one-to-one with students: supervising, coaching, mentoring and personal tutoring*. Key Guides for Effective Teaching in HE. Abingdon: Routledge.

Wood, D., Bruner, J.S. and Ross, G. 1976. The role of tutoring in problem-solving. *Journal of Child Psychology and Psychiatry and Allied Disciplines* 17: 89–100.

Wood, D.F. 2003. ABC of learning and teaching in medicine: problem-based learning. *BMJ* 325: 328–330.

Yale, A.T. 2019. The personal tutor–student relationship: student expectations and experiences of personal tutoring in higher education. *Journal of Further and Higher Education* 43: 533–544.

Zachary, L.J. and Fischler, L.A. 2009. *The mentee's guide: making mentoring work for you*. San Francisco, CA: Jossey-Bass.

Index

A Levels 29–30, 32
academic calendar 37–39
academic misconduct 123, 179
academic shock 147
academic tutoring 135, 138–139; see also personal tutors
academies 25
access 149; see also widening participation
access and participation plans 17, 180
accommodation 45, 180
accreditation 70, 162–163, 170
active learning 89
Advance HE (AHE) 7, 162–163, 164, 180; surveys 14, 158; UKPSF 12, 169, 170
after-Dennis model 72–74
aims 74–75, 180
alternative providers 5, 180
anonymous marking 120–122
applications 36
approaches to learning 45–46, 60–61, 180
Areas of activity of UKPSF 12
Aristotle 88
assessment 7, 55, 59, 109–131, 180; anonymous marking 120–122; constructive alignment 71, 72; criterion-referenced 113–114, 182; definition of 110, 111; Dennis model 74; evaluation distinction 155; formative 71, 101, 114, 115, 126, 128, 130, 184; learning outcomes 77; methods 116, 117; norm-referenced 113–114, 188; online 101; preparation of learners for 127–128; resources 129–131; self-assessment 124, 126; student surveys 157, 160; summative 71, 114, 115, 124, 125, 126, 192; synoptic 98, 192; terminology 111; UK Professional Standards Framework 111; see also examinations; feedback; marking
assessment criteria 111, 115, 119–120, 181
assessment tasks 111, 181
assimilation 45, 181
asynchronous online teaching 94, 100, 181
attainment gaps 17, 149, 181
audio-visual aids 90
Ausubel, David 50
autonomy 58–59, 60
awards 155, 170–171, 173, 177

baccalaureates 31, 40
bachelor's degrees 10, 64, 118
backwards design 72
Baillie, C. 97
Barnard, R. 165

205

INDEX

behaviourism 43
beliefs 47–49, 59
bias 120
Biggs, John 51, 54
black Asian and minority ethnic (BAME) students 17; *see also* ethnic groups
blended learning 7, 17–18, 100–101, 181
Bloom taxonomy 78
Boud, D. 97
boundaries 141
Bradbury, H. 165
Bruner, Jerome 54
BTEC Nationals 31, 32
bursaries 36–37
Butcher, C.: course content 52; course design models 72; curriculum 63–64; e-learning 100; learning 46; learning outcomes 75, 78, 186; teaching methods 83

careers services 136, 146
case-based learning (CBL) 53, 54, 84, 95–96, 106
Cathedrals Group 35, 42
challenge 54–55, 59
city technology colleges 25
class sizes 7
cognitivism 44
colleges 24, 29, 31
collusion 123
communities of practice 56
community schools 25
competition 13, 35
compulsory schooling 23–28, 181–182
confidentiality 142, 168
constructive alignment 51, 71–72, 79, 182
constructivism 44–45, 46, 50, 51, 60, 182
content: Dennis model 74; lectures 85–86; structure 52–53, 59
continuing professional development (CPD) 165, 166–167, 171
core knowledge of UKPSF 12

course context 50–56
courses 66, 182; approval 66–71; changing 78; course design 63, 71–78, 80, 154–155; learning outcomes 77; *see also* programmes
coursework 111, 182
COVID-19 pandemic 18, 101, 104
creativity 65
credits/credit ratings 8, 66–67, 68–70, 182, 187
criterion-referenced assessment 113–114, 182
critical friends 162
culture shock 147
curriculum 7, 62–81, 183; course approval 66–71; course design 71–78; definition of 63–64; progression 64–66; relevance 51
curriculum model of support 134, 144
customers, students as 37

data protection 142
Davies, C. 97
Davis, C.L. 165
Dearing Report (1997) 8, 11, 34, 51, 183
deep approach to learning 45–46, 180, 183
Dennick, R. 89
Dennis model 72–74, 154–155
Department of the Economy (Northern Ireland) 6
devolved powers 3, 6, 23
diagnostic assessment 114, 183
disability 15–16, 47; assessment 122; support 144, 149–150, 151; virtual learning environments 57; widening participation 149
disciplinary groups 164
discrimination 15, 16
dissertations 84, 98–100, 108
diversity 15, 16–17, 19, 132, 134, 149, 183
doctoral degrees 10, 64
Doto, F.X. 97
dyslexia 122

206

INDEX

e-learning 94–95, 100
Earwaker, J. 133–134
engagement 57, 87, 91, 141, 155, 157, 161
England 3, 23; funding 6; GCSEs 27, 28; National Curriculum 26, 40; polytechnics 34, 189; post-compulsory education 29; quality assurance 9; scale of higher education 5; TEF 11; tuition fees 8; universities 33; widening participation 17
English-language proficiency 147–148
Entwistle, N. 45, 48
environment 56–58, 60, 74
equality 15–16, 19, 149, 183
Equality Act (2010) 15–16, 122
ethical approval 123
ethnic groups 16, 17, 149
evaluation 74, 155, 157–162
examinations 111, 113, 117, 183; A Levels 29; exam boards 39, 127; feedback 125; misconduct 123; mock 128; schools 27, 28; writing exam questions 128–129; *see also* assessment
Exley, K. 89, 91, 93, 99
expectations 37; feedback 125; learning outcomes 77; online learning 101; personal tutoring 142; student surveys 157, 160; support 134
experiential learning 53–54, 59, 97
external examiners 127, 128, 156, 184

facilitation skills 92–93
false authorship 123
feed-forward 71, 126
feedback 55–56, 60, 116–119, 123–126, 155, 184; constructive alignment 71; continuing professional development 166–167; course approval 67; dealing with 166; definition of 110, 111; formative assessment 114, 115; interim evaluations 160; interpreting 165; online learning 101; practical

classes 98; resources 129–130; student surveys 157–159; 360-degree 163–164, 193; timing of 122; triangulation 162; UK Professional Standards Framework 111
Fischler, L.A. 167–168
Fitzpatrick, M. 165
flipped classrooms 88–89, 101, 102, 166, 184
flying faculty 4
focus groups 159, 165
formative assessment 71, 101, 114, 115, 126, 128, 130, 184
foundation schools 25
Framework for Higher Education Qualifications in England, Wales and Northern Ireland (FHEQ) 9–10, 30, 64, 184
Framework for Qualifications of Higher Education Institutions in Scotland (FQHEIS) 9–10, 64, 184
free schools 25
funding 6, 7, 20, 24–26, 34–35
further education (FE) 24, 29, 31–32
Future Learn 18

General Certificate of Secondary Education (GCSE) 27–28
George, J.H. 97
Gibbs, G. 55
grading 111, 116–118, 121, 184
graduate outcomes 43
Graduate Outcomes Survey 158–159
graduation 136, 146
grammar schools 25
grants 36–37
ground rules 93, 185
groups: problem-based learning 96; small-group teaching 57, 82, 91–95, 126
GuildHE 35, 42
gym membership metaphor 37

Haines, C. 124
hierarchy of needs 49, 56, 57

INDEX

higher education (HE) 3, 33–39; expansion of 5–6, 13, 34; history of 33–36; marketisation of 13; resources 41–42
Higher Education Academy (HEA) 169
Higher Education Funding Council for Wales (HEFCW) 6
higher education institutions (HEIs) 3, 185; awards 155, 170, 177; competition 13; funding 7; league tables 14–15, 19; prestigious 16–17; statistics 4–5; technology 17–18; types of 35–36
Higher Education Statistics Agency (HESA) 4, 13, 158–159
Higher National Certificates (HNCs) 10, 31, 32
Higher National Diplomas (HNDs) 10, 31, 32
Highers (Scotland) 30–31
Hughes, G. 145
humanism 44

icebreakers 95, 185
in-course support 136, 138–146
inclusion 15, 19, 149, 183
inclusive teaching 16, 149, 150, 185
induction 136, 137–138, 185; international students 147; new teachers 153; professional support services 144; student beliefs 48–49
institutional awards 155, 170, 177
interactivity 90
interim evaluations 159–160, 165
international English Language Testing System (IELTS) 148
International Student Barometer (ISB) 14, 159, 173
international students 5, 16, 47, 92; non-native English speakers 147–148; support for 132, 144, 146–147, 151; tuition fees 8; *see also* transnational education
iterative constructive alignment 72

John Hopkins University 80–81

Keele University 172
key stages 26–27, 186
knowledge: constructive alignment 71, 72; knowledge exchange 6, 7, 186; prior 50, 53, 59; progression 65; student beliefs 47–48; troublesome 85; UKPSF 12
Kolb, David 53

language shock 147
late submission 122
Lave, J. 56
league tables 14–15, 19
learning 6, 43–61; active 89; approaches to 45–46, 60–61, 180; assessment 110, 114; constructivism 44–45, 50; course context 50–56; learner autonomy 58–59, 60; learning environment 56–57, 60, 74; learning styles 52–53; resources 58, 60; student characteristics 46–50, 59; support for 57–58, 60; *see also* online learning
learning circles 156, 163
learning logs 84
learning outcomes 9, 59, 74–78, 186; assessment 113–114, 115; course approval 67; course context 51; Dennis model 74; iterative constructive alignment 72; lectures 87; resources 80–81; small-group teaching 92; student surveys 157, 160; teaching methods 84
lecture capture 88–89, 90, 186
lectures 82, 84, 85–90, 102–103, 124
level descriptors 65, 186–187
loans 36–37
local-authority-maintained schools 25
Lochtie, D. 134
low-income students 16–17, 149

Macfarlane-Dick, D. 124
maintenance grants and loans 36–37
major changes (to courses) 67, 68, 78, 187

208

INDEX

marketing 13
marking 111, 113, 116–122, 187; assessment criteria 119–120; external examiners 127; moderation 126; resources 130–131; rubrics 115, 120; software 125
Marton, F. 45, 48
Maslow, Abraham 49, 56, 57
Maslow's hierarchy of needs 49, 59
Massive Online Open Courses (MOOCs) 18, 105, 164, 174
master's degrees 10, 64, 98, 118
May, S.A. 83
mental health issues 141
mentors 154, 162, 167–168, 173
MillionPlus Group 35, 42
minor changes (to courses) 67, 68, 78, 187
misconduct 123, 179
mock exams 128
moderation 111, 113, 126, 187
modularisation 38, 187
modules 66, 187; assessment 114, 192; choice 52; course approval 67, 68; credits/credit ratings 69, 182; learning outcomes 77; student surveys 157
motivation 47, 49–50, 52, 59, 86–87, 124
multi-media content 100

national awards 171, 177
National Curriculum 25, 26–27, 40, 188
National Student Survey (NSS) 13–14, 112, 143, 158, 161, 174–175, 188
National Union of Students (NUS) 120, 175; see also students' unions
Newcastle University 77
newsletters 164–165
Nicol, D.J. 124
non-native English speakers 147–148
norm-referenced assessment 113–114, 188

Northern Ireland 3, 23; Equality Commission 16; funding 6; GCSEs 27, 28; National Curriculum 40; polytechnics 34, 189; post-compulsory education 29; quality assurance 9; scale of higher education 5; TEF 11; tuition fees 8; universities 33

Office for Students (OfS) 6, 11, 17
Office of Qualifications & Examinations Regulation (Ofqual) 28
online discussions 84
online learning 17–18, 19, 94–95, 100–101, 103–106, 181, 188; see also virtual learning environments
Oxford Brookes University 6

part-time students 16
pastoral model of support 133, 134, 138
peer evaluation 155–156
peer review/observation 163, 175–176
Penn State 175
personal tutoring system 133, 138–144, 188
personal tutors 132, 135, 138–144, 150, 188; challenges 140–142; confidentiality 142; pre-entry guidance 137; role of 139–140; senior tutors 135, 143–144, 191; student lifecycle 136
physical environment 56, 57, 60
Pitt, E. 120
plagiarism 123, 131
Pokorny, H. 127
polytechnics 6, 34, 189
portfolios 161–162, 176
post-compulsory education 28–31, 40, 189
Postgraduate Research Experience Survey (PRES) 158, 172
postgraduate students 14, 36, 82, 158
Postgraduate Taught Experience Survey (PTES) 158, 172
Potter, J. 170

209

INDEX

practical classes 53, 82, 84, 96–98, 106, 124, 126
pre-entry guidance 135–137, 150
pre-university education 23–33, 39–40
preparation: assessment 127–128; online learning 100; small-group teaching 93–94
prior knowledge 50, 53, 59
private schools 25–26
problem-based learning (PBL) 53, 54, 84, 95–96, 106
professional bodies 66–67, 189
professional development 153–178
professional model of support 133, 134
professional, statutory and regulatory bodies (PSRBs) 70–71, 189
professional support services 134, 135, 136, 144–145, 190
professional values of UKPSF 12
programme specifications 9, 73, 190
programmes 66, 68, 190; *see also* courses
progression 64–66, 190
projects 84, 98–100, 108, 117
Public Sector Equality Duty 15
pupil referral units (PRUs) 24, 41

QS World University Rankings 3, 20
Qualification Frameworks 8, 9–10, 30, 64, 184
qualifications 9–10, 41, 64, 162–163; changes in 33; further education 31–32; post-compulsory education 29–30; teaching 11–13
quality assurance 7, 8–11, 19–20, 154, 155–162, 190
Quality Assurance Agency (QAA) 8–11, 64; assessment 110, 119; level descriptors 65, 186–187; subject benchmark statements 70
Quality Code 8, 190
quality enhancement 154, 162–165, 190

rankings 3, 14–15, 20
reading lists 86

recognition 154, 155, 168–171
redbrick universities 33–34
reflective practice 156, 165, 191
reflective practitioners 156, 165, 191
regulation 6–7, 20, 141
relevance 51–52, 59
reliability 115
research 6, 7
resources 58, 60, 67, 159
Robbins Report (1963) 34, 191
role modelling 87
role play 84
rubrics 115, 120
Russell Group Universities 35, 42
Ryan, J. 165

Säljö, R. 45, 48
Salmon, Gilly 95
satisfaction 14, 112, 155, 157, 158, 161
scaffolding 54–55
schema 45, 191
schools 23–28, 181–182
Scotland 3, 23; applications 36; bursaries 36–37; cap on student numbers 35; funding 6; National Curriculum 40; Nationals 27, 28; post-compulsory education 29, 30–31; quality assurance 9; scale of higher education 5; TEF 11; tuition fees 8; universities 33; widening access 149
Scottish Funding Council 6
Seattle University 174
self-actualisation 49, 56
self-assessment 124, 126
self-esteem 49, 56, 57, 124
semesters 37–38, 191
seminars 84, 91–94, 106–107, 124, 126
senior tutors 135, 143–144, 191
Silva-Fletcher, A. 83
Simpson, C. 55
simulations 84
situational learning theories 44

INDEX

sixth-forms 24, 29, 31
small-group teaching 57, 82, 91–95, 126
social constructivism 45, 54
social environment 56
social events 137, 138
social learning theories 44
social media 137
Staff and Educational Development Association Professional Development Framework (SEDA PDF) 163, 170
staff-student committees 161
Starr, J. 167–168
Stork, A. 138
student-centred approach 44, 191
students 36–37; background 47, 59; beliefs 47–49, 59; diversity 16–17; learner autonomy 58–59, 60; motivation 49–50, 59; prior knowledge 50, 59; quality assurance 155; student lifecycle 134, 136; student numbers 5–6; student representation 161; support for 57–58, 60, 132–152; surveys 13–14, 20, 112, 143, 157–162, 174–175, 188
students' unions 138, 145–146, 170, 192; *see also* National Union of Students
subject benchmark statements 8, 10–11, 43, 66–67, 70, 192
summative assessment 71, 114, 115, 124, 125, 126, 192
supervision 82, 98–100, 108
support 57–58, 60, 132–152; induction 137–138; models of 133–135; new teachers 153; personal tutoring 138–144; pre-entry guidance 135–137; professional support services 134, 135, 136, 144–145, 190; progression onwards 146; specific students 146–150; students' unions 144–145
surface approach to learning 45–46, 180, 192

surveys 13–14, 20, 21–22, 172, 174–175, 188; assessment 109–110, 111; curriculum 62–63; professional development 153–154; quality assurance 157–162; support 132–133, 143; teaching 82–83
synchronous online teaching 94, 100, 192
synoptic assessment 98, 192
synthesis 65

T Levels 30, 40
tablets 90
Tang, C. 54
teacher-centred approach 44, 192
teaching 6, 82–108; Dennis model 74; funding 7; inclusive 16, 149, 150, 185; portfolios 161–162; student surveys 157–158
Teaching and Learning Observation College (TLOC) 163
Teaching Excellence and Student Outcomes Framework (TEF) 11, 193
teaching qualifications 11–13
technology 7, 17–18, 88–89, 90–91, 108; *see also* online learning; virtual learning environments
terms 37–39, 193
tests 111, 193; *see also* assessment; examinations
Thomas, L. 145
360-degree feedback 163–164, 193
threshold concepts 52, 53, 61, 75, 85
Timm, H. 100
Tjan, A. 168
Tomorrow's Professor 177–178
training 34, 140, 156, 162–163
transnational education (TNE) 3–4, 6, 20, 193; application process 36; course approval 67; holiday dates 38–39; student support 146–147; teaching qualifications 13; tuition fees 8; *see also* international students
transparency 115, 119
triangulation 155, 162, 193

211

INDEX

tuition fees 7–8, 34, 37
Turner, R. 170
tutorials 84, 91–94, 106–107, 124, 126

UCAS tariff 30, 194
UK Professional Standards Framework (UKPSF) 1–2, 164, 168–170, 172–173, 194; assessment 111; dimensions 12; fellowships 154, 162–163, 169–170 units 66, 187, 194; assessment 192; course approval 67; credits/credit ratings 69, 182; learning outcomes 77; student surveys 157
Universities and Colleges Admission Service (UCAS) 30, 36, 42, 194
University Alliance 35, 42
University College Dublin 80
University of Adelaide 80
University of Bristol 80
University of Cambridge 3, 33, 36, 134
University of Derby 172
University of Leeds 172
University of Nottingham 4, 141, 143, 163, 175
University of Oxford 3, 33, 36, 134, 177
University of Plymouth 176
University of Sheffield 174
University of Warwick 163, 172, 177
University of Westminster 177
University of York 177

validity 115
values 12, 77
Vanderbilt University 81
virtual learning environments (VLEs) 7, 18, 57, 74, 188, 194; interim evaluations 159, 160; lectures 88–89; peer evaluation 156; reading lists 86; small-group teaching 94; *see also* online learning
voluntary schools 25
Vygotsky, Lev 54

Wales 3, 23; funding 6; GCSEs 27, 28; National Curriculum 26, 40; polytechnics 34, 189; post-compulsory education 29; quality assurance 9; scale of higher education 5; TEF 11; tuition fees 8; universities 33
Walker, B. 138
Warwick International Higher Education Academy (WIHEA) 163
Welsh Higher Education Credit Framework (WHECF) 65
Wenger, E. 56
widening participation (WP) 16–17, 149, 152, 194
Winstone, N. 120
workload 69–70, 157

Zachary, L.J. 167–168
zone of proximal development (ZPD) by Vygotsky 54